MORE FOUL DEEDS AND SUSPICIOUS DEATHS IN WAKEFIELD

'FOUL DEEDS AND SUSPICIOUS DEATHS' Series

Foul Deeds and Suspicious Deaths series explores in detail crimes of passion, brutal murders, grisly deeds and foul misdemeanours. From Victorian street crime, to more modern murder where passion, jealousy, or social depravation brought unexpected violence to those involved. From mysterious death to murder and manslaughter, the books are a fascinating insight into not only those whose lives are forever captured by the suffering they endured, but also into the society that moulded and shaped their lives. Each book takes you on a journey into the darker and unknown side of the area.

Other titles in the series

Foul Deeds and Suspicious Deaths in Blackburn & Hyndburn, Stephen Greenhalgh
1 903425 18 2 . £9.99

Foul Deeds and Suspicious Deaths In and Around Chesterfield, Geoffrey Sadler
1 903425 30 1 . £9.99

Foul Deeds and Suspicious Deaths In Leeds, David Goodman
1 903425 08 5 . £9.99

Foul Deeds and Suspicious Deaths In Nottingham, Kevin Turton
1 903425 35 2 . £9.99

Foul Deeds and Suspicious Deaths In and Around Rotherham, Kevin Turton
1 903425 27 1 . £9.99

Foul Deeds and Suspicious Deaths In and Around The Tees, Maureen Anderson
1 903425 26 3 . £9.99

Foul Deeds and Suspicious Deaths In Wakefield, Kate Taylor
1 903425 07 7 . £9.99

Foul Deeds and Suspicious Deaths In York, Keith Henson
1 903425 33 6 . £9.99

Foul Deeds & Suspicious Deaths on the Yorkshire Coast, Alan Whitworth
1 903425 01 8 . £9.99

Other Local Books

The Making of The West Yorkshire Landscape, Anthony Silson
1 903425 31 x . £9.99

Trams Around Dewsbury & Wakefield, Norman Ellis
1 903425 40 9 . £9.99

Please contact us via any of the methods below for more information or a catalogue.
WHARNCLIFFE BOOKS
47 Church Street – Barnsley – South Yorkshire – S70 2AS
Tel: 01226 734555 – 734222 Fax: 01226 734438
E-mail: enquiries@pen-and-sword.co.uk – Website: www.wharncliffebooks.co.uk

More Foul Deeds and Suspicious Deaths in

WAKEFIELD

KATE TAYLOR

Series Editor
Brian Elliott

Wharncliffe Books

First Published in 2003 by
Wharncliffe Books
an imprint of
Pen and Sword Books Limited,
47 Church Street, Barnsley,
South Yorkshire. S70 2AS

For up-to-date information on other titles produced under the
Wharncliffe imprint, please telephone or write to:

Wharncliffe Books
FREEPOST
47 Church Street
Barnsley
South Yorkshire S70 2BR
Telephone (24 hours): 01226 - 734555

ISBN: 1-903425-48-4

A CIP catalogue record of this book is available from the
British Library

Cover illustration: *Back:* Crofton Churchyard, *Kate Taylor*

Printed in the United Kingdom by
CPI UK

CONTENTS

Introduction

This volume focuses on foul deeds in the nineteenth and twentieth centuries. Some references to earlier murders and other capital offences are to be found in an account published in 1867 of the executions in York from 1379 onwards.[1] There we find that one Robert de Fleury, who was fifty and a Wakefield man, was hanged in 1574 for wounding Baron de Cavallo near Shipton; his body was handed over for dissection. In 1578 William Henry de Boyle was hanged for the murder of his servant, Sarah Robson of Wakefield, by strangling her with his whiplash in his bedroom, in front of his wife and daughter; his body was brought to 'Wakefield Common' and hung in chains as an awful warning. Other executions of Wakefield people recorded in the book relate to Luddite activity, sheep stealing, and stealing a horse. However, forty year old John Senior is noted as the first man in the county to be hung for defrauding his creditors; his execution was in 1813.

I have included one case of rape and one of attempted rape among these accounts. Few cases of rape were in the past brought successfully to trial. This was not because rape did not happen. Rather it was because it was both difficult to prove and a severe ordeal for the woman to give evidence. It seems, too, that at least one Assize judge cautioned the Grand Jury against accepting a bill of rape. In 1837 the judge at York advised that unless the case was clear, the charge should be thrown out and perhaps one of assault might be substituted, but that 'such cases are extremely unpleasant to investigate and they in no slight degree offend the morals of the community'. It was at those Assizes that three young men from Ossett, John Milnes, George Kemp, and Walter Carr, had been awaiting trial for the rape of one Mary Stuart but Mary failed to appear and the charges seem to have been dropped.

It was the task of the Grand Jury, made up of men of considerable substance from across Yorkshire, to determine whether a case should be heard or not and whether the original charge should be amended. They might decide that the charge of manslaughter should be substituted for the original one of murder. They might also decide that the evidence was too slight to warrant the case being heard at all. This may well have happened when James Bedford awaited trial for causing the death of a fellow miner in 1836 (Chapter 3).

I have also included two cases where death seems to have been self-inflicted or at least where no other party was involved. They provide an interesting contrast. There can have been no doubt that Albert Goodall (Chapter 20), a somewhat pathetic figure, took his own life; he left a suicide note and the reasons for his decision seem clear. On the other hand Colonel Thomas Chadwick (Chapter 47) was not, it was strongly felt in the culture of the time, the type to kill himself and the coroner worked hard to secure an open verdict.

Coroners' inquests were opened shortly after a sudden death was known. The body was normally to hand for the members of the jury to see. Although recommendations had been made in 1935 that the practice of the jury naming the killer should cease so that the matter could be left to the police and the criminal courts, it went on until 1977, finally coming to and end following the Brodrick Report of 1971. The practice of juries adding a rider to their verdict ceased only in 1980.[2]

Until well into the twentieth century it was normal for inquests to take place in the nearest public house to the place where the subject died or the body was found. The corpse was brought to the inquest to be viewed by the jurors. It may seem curious that three inquests referred to in this volume took place in three different public houses in the Wakefield area, each named *The Graziers*. The name reflects the fact that drovers brought livestock long distances on foot to the market in Wakefield and spent a little time letting them graze and fatten up in the fields surrounding the town.

In the course of reading so many inquests, one becomes familiar with some of the coroners. In preparing this volume, I have enjoyed encounters in particular with Pelham Maitland, who became deputy coroner in 1885 and coroner from 1900 until his death in 1918, who was given to an element of bullying where less articulate witnesses were concerned and who quite regularly made criticism of the manners or morals of those he encountered. Following an inquest into the death of a Crofton man in 1903, for example, he censured the couple who had given him overnight hospitality, referring (it is hard to judge why) to the 'disgraceful manner in which they conducted their house and neglected their children'. In 1908 he told a bereaved husband that he had 'not shown the anxiety' for his wife that he should have done. Other of his remarks can be found in some of the accounts provided here.

Until it became legal in 1967 to terminate pregnancies, at least in certain circumstances, many women died as a result of 'back street' abortions. Coroners might condemn those who assisted the unfortunate women and suggest that they should be found and prosecuted, but this was always easier said than done. Unwanted babies have always been a problem and were – and perhaps still are – the most vulnerable members of society. An overview of murder and manslaughter in the past would be unbalanced without the inclusion of accounts of their deaths and, whilst many more were recorded in the centuries under review, I have included a significant few here.

Almost every case is of interest to the local historian for the light it sheds on past ways of life. One learns, for example, that in 1903 it was possible to conduct one's business as a commission agent, or bookmaker, by standing for a period each day on a street corner (Chapter 23) or that labourers working on a new railway were quite ready to take an hour off work when two of their number began a fight and that they had a fair notion of the rules of combat (Chapter 7). One learns, too, of the practice of sending an identifiable beer jug to the local hostelry to be filled and brought home (Chapter 33). Much can be learned of attitudes towards women in the period before feminist campaigning began to change perceptions In the days before the West Riding County Constabulary was established in 1856, we see the efforts of the assistant township constable (Chapter 9) to cope with a suspected crime and the absconding perpetrators.

I am grateful to John Goodchild, M Univ., for his unfailing advice on a wide range of historical points, and to the staff of the local studies department at Wakefield Library Headquarters for their ready assistance and encouragement. Thanks are due also to Brian Elliott, the General Editor of this series, for his guidance and to the staff at Wharncliffe Books.

Notes
1. *Criminal Chronology of York Castle with a register of the criminals capitally convicted and executed at the county assizes, commencing March 1 1379 to the present time.* York (1886).
2. *Jarvis on Coroners.*

CHAPTER 1

Justifiable Homicide
1831

Poaching was a sufficient problem on the Woolley Hall estate in the early 1830s for three men to spend a wintry night in 1831 watching over the game in Seckar Wood. They were Matthew Ellis, the under-keeper, and two assistants, Joseph Horbury and John Naylor.

About three o'clock on the morning of 7 January the keepers heard a gun-shot. Naylor was sent to fetch the head keeper, Francis Child. Armed with a gun, Child directed Horbury and Naylor to watch at the north side of the wood whilst he himself, with Ellis, made their way to the south side.

At the Hunting Gate, Child and Ellis found a group of men, including Joseph Appleyard, George Milner and Jonathan Westerman. Milner was carrying a gun and his comrades held heavy bludgeons. Child shouted for the two assistants to join them and bade Ellis 'stick to them'. One of the poachers responded, 'Aye and we'll stick to thee'. Appleyard urged Milner to shoot the head keeper but Child said firmly, 'If you are men, you'll not shoot'.

The poachers set off across a field with Child and Ellis following them. At the edge of the field, Child placed himself in front of the poachers and ordered them to 'Stand', whereupon Appleyard punched him in the face and his companions set about him with their bludgeons knocking him to the ground. Child sat up and held his gun in front of his face to ward off the blows. Milner held a gun to Child's head and one of the poachers said, 'Blow his brains out'. Child knocked the gun away. It went off and he heard Ellis cry out that he had been shot. Then one of the poachers struck at Child's own gun with a bludgeon. It too went off wounding Appleyard in the right leg. Ellis was knocked down and Milner shot him in the thigh. Milner turned to flee and

Ellis shot him in the spine. Somehow, too, Westerman was injured.

When at last Horbury and Naylor arrived on the scene they found both the keepers and all three injured poachers sprawled on the ground. They fetched a cart and the poachers were taken to the *Wentworth Arms* whilst the keepers struggled behind them on foot.

A Wakefield surgeon, Joseph Bennett, then of Almshouse Lane, was summoned. He said that the only hope of saving Appleyard's life – and a slender one at that – was to amputate the injured leg. Despite the operation, Appleyard died later the same day. Meanwhile his fellow poachers were taken to the House of Correction in Wakefield.

On the following day, Saturday 8 January, coroner Thomas Lee conducted an inquest into Appleyard's death. Rather than a verdict of 'accidental death', the jury pronounced the killing as 'justifiable homicide'.

Both Milner and Westerman remained bedridden at the gaol. The following Wednesday four magistrates, Sir John

The house on the left, overlooking the village green in Woolley and pictured in 2003, was formerly the Wentworth Arms *to which the injured poachers were taken.* The author

Lister Kaye, John Blayes, Daniel Gaskell and John Maude, took the unusual step of going there to examine them. Child and Ellis were taken to the hearing in one of Godfrey Wentworth's carriages. The poachers were committed for trial at the Assizes on a charge of being out at night armed for the purpose of taking game.

At the trial, which took place at York on 4 April, it was said that both poachers were still suffering from the effects of their wounds and that one of them would be maimed for life. They were found guilty. Westerman was sentenced to eighteen months' imprisonment at Wakefield and Milner was sentenced to two years. Both were to do 'such labour as they were capable of pursuing'.

CHAPTER 2

A Horrific Fall
1834

J oseph Swailes of Ossett Streetside died on 2 March 1834 as a result of injuries he sustained when he fell – or was thrown – over a four-foot wall and down a drop of almost nine yards. The inquest jury returned a verdict of murder against three persons unknown, but questions at the inquest showed that there was some uncertainty about the actual circumstances.

Swailes was a spinner at Sandy Mill. On Saturday 1 March he had gone to Earlsheaton. On his way home he called, at about 5.30 pm, at the beer shop there run by Isaac Preston. He stayed a couple of hours and drank at least two pints of ale. For some of the time there he was in the company of four members of Dewsbury Band, Thomas Coldwell, Robert and Isaac Senior, and William Turner. The bandsmen left before Swailes, however, to continue their way to Dewsbury.

Swailes claimed that, as he walked along the then-new road in the great cutting, he was attacked by three men. He was thrown over the wall, his head hit the buttress of the new road as he fell and he then landed on the old road many feet below. For a couple of hours he lay, unable to move. Then he crawled to the house of James Lumb, a coal miner, some 120 yards away, and stumbled in at about 10 pm, bleeding profusely from injuries to the back of his head. Lumb fetched his neighbours, John Stocks and his wife, and sent for Swailes' wife. Between them they helped Swailes to his home. Dr J Smith was summoned. Swailes died the following day. Although he spoke of himself as 'a murdered man', he was unable to name his assailants.

An inquest was held the following day at the *Waggon and Horses*. Dr Smith was present and greatly put out because some of Swailes's friends had insisted that a Mr G Greenwood

The lower part of Dewsbury cutting in 2003. The author

be present at the post-mortem. The body was examined not only by Dr Smith but also by Dr William Wood Wiseman of Ossett Green. In fact a dispute between the two medical men led to letters from both of them to the *Wakefield and Dewsbury Journal* but both were agreed that Swailes died from a ruptured bowel caused either by a blow to his abdomen or by the fall itself.

But were there ever any assailants? The question arose first as to whether Swailes had been drunk and had simply fallen in his befuddled state. Isaac Preston agreed that he had been 'fresh' when he left the beer house but not exactly the worse for wear. So did he suffer from epilepsy? Swailes had worked for twenty years for William Rhodes of Earlsheaton and Rhodes told the inquest that he had never known him to have a fit. However, Sarah Robinson, the wife of a local tailor, claimed that he had been subject to fits. If, however, he really had dropped from the new road, there was the question of how he had got over the high wall at its side. No arrests were made and no more can be known.

CHAPTER 3

The Incautious Use of a Candle
1836

James Bedford was an experienced miner. He had worked in coal mines from boyhood and, by now in his mid- thirties and living at Lee Fair, he had undertaken work as a sinker and a borer as well as at the coal face. When his 'incautious use of a candle' led to the deaths of three boys, he was working as a 'hanger-on' (fastening the corves, or wagon-loads of coal on to the rope which drew them up the shaft) at the Bull Pit, Alverthorpe. The pit was a part of the colliery of Joshua Smithson. In partnership with George Broadhead and David Brooke, Bedford had also contracted to undertake the hurrying at the pit (bringing the wagons from the coal face to the shaft) and for this he employed a number of lads.

But experienced though he was, Bedford's ill-judgment caused the fatal explosion which happened at about twelve noon on Saturday, 13 August 1836. There were only sixteen men working underground at the time but there were also eight boys, including Bedford's hurriers. Because many of the men were away, there was insufficient work for the hurriers to do and Bedford had sent them to 'get' coal themselves with the knowledge, it was said, of the master. Towards mid-day Bedford had gone to help one of his boys, young Benjamin Scott, taking his candle with him.

Although safety lamps were available at the Bull Pit, and indeed Scott was using one, colliers still preferred to work with candles, despite the danger from the naked flame, and witnesses reckoned that in some parts of the pit they were safe enough. But not in the bank where Scott was working. Only the previous day, another of the colliers, Joseph Berry, had warned Bedford against taking his candle into that section of the pit. But Bedford had paid no heed.

The flame ignited a build-up of firedamp (a mixture of hydrocarbons, primarily methane), causing the explosion. Three boys died immediately and other boys and men were injured.

An inquest was held into the death of one of the boys, seventeen-year old John Pickford, the following day. Joseph Berry was one of the witnesses. He told how he had been working in the bank next to Scott's. On hearing the explosion he had lain down and managed to escape unhurt. There was a fire in Scott's bank and he found the boy there alive but burnt. The second witness was George Longley, of Alverthorpe, one of the bottom stewards. He affirmed that there was good ventilation in the pit and explained that miners worked better with candles than with safety lamps. Bedford did not have a safety lamp. William Thomas Andrew, from Ossett, another bottom steward, claimed that the pit was in a good state and described Bedford as a 'steady man'. Bedford, he said, had been as much exposed to danger himself as anyone else.

Low Laithes from Lindle Hill in 2002, showing the landscape where the Bull Pit was. The author

The jury found that Pickford's death resulted from 'suffocation by foul air produced by the effects of the explosion of firedamp caused by the incautious use of a candle or other light'. No blame was laid directly on Bedford.

However, there was a second inquest the following day into the deaths of two more boys. Berry gave evidence again and this time spoke of how, on the day before the explosion, he had warned Bedford against bringing a candle into that part of the pit. Joseph Scott, of Potovens, who was the father of Benjamin, explained that he had talked with his son after the explosion. He had gone down the pit about an hour after the explosion to look for three missing people. He had gone into the bank where Benjamin had been working and found the remains of the candle there.

This time the jury brought a verdict of manslaughter against Bedford. Shortly afterwards he was committed to York Castle to await trial at the Assizes on charges of 'killing and slaying'.

Clearly there were those who thought that the long stay in prison awaiting trial was entirely inappropriate. An application was made on his behalf to the county magistrates for bail.

Their response was simply that it lay outside their power. The *Wakefield Herald* reported that a further application was to be made to 'the judges' and that bail would probably be granted. I have found no record as to whether it was or not.

Bedford's case was on the charge sheet for the Lent Assizes in 1837. Evidently the judge was concerned by it as he singled it out for the attention of the Grand Jury whose task it was to determine whether a case should actually come to trial. In his address at the opening of the Assizes, the judge observed, 'This is a case which will require very close attention because the party charged may have taken the candle very innocently, but if he was told to take a safety lamp and refused or neglected to do so, and that refusal or negligence caused an explosion, then the man would become answerable for his conduct.' It seems that the Grand Jury decided that there was insufficient evidence to secure a conviction and the case was dropped.

CHAPTER 4

A Case of the Ordinary Kind
1836

A death following a fight in a public house was deemed 'one of the ordinary kind' when Joseph Haigh was tried at York Assizes in March 1837, for the manslaughter of twenty-three year old Robert Waller at Tingley Moor in September 1836.

The 'squabble' occurred on Saturday evening, 17 September. It was the time of Lee Fair. Horsefairs at West Ardsley are of ancient origin going back to a charter, probably of Henry I, and were earlier held on the feast of the Assumption and the feast of the nativity of Mary the mother of Jesus, 15 August and 8 September. By 1837, however, they were held on 24 August and 17 September. They drew – and still draw – horse traders from all over the country. For the local folk they provided a day out and an excuse for a pub crawl.

Public houses in the area took on extra staff for the occasions. Much of the evidence at the inquest into Waller's death was given by George Moxon of Stanley, who was a wheelwright and joiner by trade but who was lending a hand at the *White Bear* at Tingley on the Saturday night. Further evidence came from William Rooley, a cloth drawer from Tingley Moor, who was the son-in-law of the landlord, Joseph Barras, and who was also staffing the pub that evening, and from William Clough, a cloth dresser from Morley who was also 'waiting'.

Waller, who was from Morley, came with his friends to the *White Bear* after visiting the *Bull's Head*. There the group had already harassed the servant of West Ardsley farmer, John Hodgson. At the *White Bear* Waller had a pint of ale in the kitchen before going to an upstairs room where there was already a good crowd of drinkers including Joseph Haigh. He

A postcard view of Lee Fair in the early twentieth century. Norman Ellis. Collection

picked a quarrel with what was described as 'a little boy' of perhaps fourteen years of age (the boy was never more fully identified), took off his coat and waistcoat and proposed to fight the lad. He struck him but others pushed him down and told him to 'be quiet'. He 'knocked about a bit' and offered to fight anyone in the room. With the help of others, Moxon, who had brought more ale to the room, locked Waller up in a smaller room nearby. Moxon told the gathering that he would bring no more orders upstairs. The majority of them then went down to the tap room although Haigh and his friends remained upstairs.

After about thirty minutes, William Rooley freed Waller and he went downstairs to the 'low room' to join his associates where they continued drinking. He was just emerging from this room when Haigh came downstairs. They met in the passageway. Haigh said, 'Thou art a shabby fellow to strike at the boy in such a manner. How could thou fashion?' At this, Waller struck Haigh. Haigh pushed him off but Waller swore that he would fight him. Both went into the tap room where other men from Morley were gathered. Joseph Dickinson, of Morley, a weaver and friend of Waller claimed that he tried to stop the fight. His friend was fond of fighting when drunk, he said, and he was very drunk then. Joseph Scott, a West Ardsley farmer, who was with Haigh and was married to Haigh's sister, seems to have urged the two men on. Both stripped off their coats, waistcoats, neck-cloths and hats. Haigh felled Waller with the first blow. Waller got up at once and was immediately knocked down again. Waller then got to his knees and seized Haigh by the thighs. Haigh struck him again, he fell forward, and, so witnesses said, died immediately.

Rooley rode off for the doctor, John Gisborne.

Gisborne and Dr Samuel Hare conducted a post-mortem examination. From their evidence is seems no wonder that

Lee Fair in 2002. The Wakefield Express.

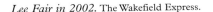

Another scene at Lee Fair in 2002. The Wakefield Express.

Waller died. He would, they said, have been dead in a few months anyway. He had an enlarged heart and diseased lungs and liver. The blow simply hastened the event.

Haigh was tried at the Assizes and found not guilty.

CHAPTER 5

A Stabbing in the Small Hours
Led to a Suicide
1837

William Swift left the *Little Bull* in Westgate at 1.40am on the morning of 25 July 1837 to make his way to his home in Thornes Lane. He was not the only man about in the centre of Wakefield at that hour. Joseph Green, a joiner, was seated on a window sill at the top of White Swan Yard when George Birkenshaw, a thirty-year old grocer, and Joseph Rhodes came up to him and invited him to walk with them to Kirkgate corner. Harriet North, out looking for her husband, was going up Warrengate. Rhodes and Birkenshaw

The junction of Warrengate and Kirkgate where the fracas took place, pictured in 2003. The author

accosted her with Green, and now too, Swift, following them. There was a fight which Green and Swift tried to stop. Rhodes and Birkenshaw then turned on Swift. Green managed to draw the attackers away.

John Stead, who was the landlord of the *Dolphin*, was woken about 2 am by all the noise and heard Swift say that he had been stabbed. He saw three other men walking away. John White Ellis, who was an apprentice to Perkins the grocer, heard Swift say, 'Joe Green, I call you to witness that he has stabbed me'.

Swift's injuries were serious. Henry Graham, an apprentice to Dr William Statter, was called out at 3 am to Swift's home where he found him sitting by the fireside. He had a deep wound to the chest cavity and a further wound to the abdomen. Graham washed and dressed the wounds and got Swift to bed. He and Statter saw him again that afternoon. Inflammation set in and for a time Swift's life was in danger.

Meanwhile Birkenshaw and Rhodes were arrested, charged with wounding with intent to kill and committed for trial at York Assizes.

But Birkenshaw was never tried. A fellow prisoner at York Castle, George Shackleton, said that Birkenshaw was deeply depressed, grieving that he had brought shame upon his family. The day he died he had had a letter from his brother. When John Noble, an undergaoler at the prison went to his cell at 7am on 1 September, he found him hanging from a window by a silk handkerchief. Noble said that he had always had a gloomy countenance. An inquest jury found that he had committed suicide while temporarily insane. What happened to Rhodes? He does not seem to have been tried at the Assizes in March 1838. Possibly he too had died. Or perhaps the Grand Jury had decided that there was insufficient evidence to bring the case to trial.

CHAPTER 6

Neglect or Natural Causes?
1840

Before Sarah Bolland died, a warrant was issued for the arrest of her husband, Joshua Bolland, a Stanley butcher and thatcher, on a charge of neglect and other ill-treatment of his family. However, by the time Bolland came before the West Riding magistrates at the Court House in Wood Street, Wakefield, on 13 January 1840, his wife had been dead for twenty-four hours. Coroner Thomas Lee and a Wakefield doctor, William Rowlandson, attended the short hearing. Rowlandson said that he 'would not have treated a dog' in the way Bolland treated his wife. The magistrates then decided to hand the whole matter over to the coroner.

It was thus at the inquest at *The Graziers* public house, Stanley, on 14 January that the sad story was told.

Sarah, who was forty-seven when she died, was Bolland's second wife. The couple had been married for about five years. Although Sarah had not been married before, she had an adult daughter, Mary Ann Schorah, who had lived at the Bollands for a short period but had left after a quarrel and who lived in January 1840 in lodgings in Boat Lane. Bolland had two children, the older of them, Jane, being just fourteen when her step-mother died.

In the summer of 1839, Sarah became ill. She was attended for a few weeks in July by Rowlandson but he had not been called in thereafter. In the last weeks of her life, Sarah was visited regularly by the vicar of Stanley, Reverend John Lister, and his evidence at the inquest was critical. He confirmed that Sarah had had no medical attention in the weeks prior to her death despite her being very ill. He said that she had complained to him of her husband's ill treatment: he had seized her by the legs and pulled her half out of bed; she had been very thirsty and asked him to bring her a drink of water, but he would not. Sarah had asked to be removed to her brother's house where she could be 'in peace', but she was not moved. One Thursday, about three weeks before her death, the vicar had called and found that Sarah's bed had not been made since the previous Sunday and the bedroom was so dirty as to be almost intolerable. He had taxed her husband over this neglect and had stayed to see the room cleaned and the bed freshly made. On the other hand, Lister said, Sarah did not lack for food, she had told him that neighbours and friends were very kind to her, and she admitted that Bolland ill-treated her only when he was intoxicated.

Was it Sarah's physical weakness, or was it her shrewish tongue that provoked Bolland? Evidence was given by Dinah Bolland, the wife of Joshua's brother, James, that she and Sarah did not get on very well. They had quarrelled when Sarah's daughter took some onions without asking from Charles Bolland's field. Dinah claimed that Bolland had begun to drink only after marrying Sarah. Dinah lived next door to Bolland and Sarah and in the first year of their

The Grazier's Inn, *Stanley, in 2003 It was at the Graziers that the inquest was held into the death of Sarah Bolland.* The author

marriage had heard Bolland give his wife a blow. She once heard Sarah cry 'Murder!'.

Charles Bolland, who was Joshua Bolland's cousin, admitted that he, too, had heard quarrelling. He lived some hundred yards away from James Bolland's house but, coming home from chapel a fortnight before Sarah's death, he had heard Bolland say that 'the Devil would have her – he had got half of her already'. He did not hear any blows, however. He admitted that his cousin had neglected Sarah and was regularly 'fresh' or the worse for drink. He had called on her after hearing the quarrelling and she told him she had had nothing but a few potatoes to eat. He went at once to get her 'some meat' and arranged for a dinner to be sent to her from his own home each day.

Others, too, gave what help they could. Harriet Wroe said at the inquest that in the three weeks prior to Sarah's death, she had gone in to make her bed each day. Although living nearby, she had never seen or heard any quarrels and Sarah had never complained to her of Bolland's treatment of her.

Sarah's daughter, Mary Ann, claimed that she dared not go to visit her mother unless she was sure that Bolland was out because he had threatened to murder her. When she was with her mother, she set two children to watch out for Bolland's coming home so that she could make her escape before he found her there. She had called on the Friday evening before Sarah died, but dared not stay long.

Joseph Tollerton, the Assistant Overseer of the Poor for the Stanley cum Wrenthorpe township, told the inquest that he had sought a warrant for the arrest of Bolland because of complaints from the neighbours about his ill-treatment of his wife. He had obtained the warrant on the Tuesday before Sarah died but had not got it signed immediately as he needed to ask Sarah herself some questions first. When he saw her, her voice was strong. She told him she would like to be separated from her husband for the little time left to her; she wanted peace and there was no peace in her present home. Tollerton gave her 2s 6d (12.5p) poor relief. He had not expected her to die as soon as she did.

But Dr William Statter, who examined Sarah's body, said that it was not at all surprising that she had died. Her heart

was enlarged and her left lung was 'one mass of disease' –
tuberculosis. Only the lower part of the right lung was clear.
She was emaciated and wasted. The lung disease was quite
sufficient to cause her death. He could find no evidence that
she had died by violence and insisted that no treatment could
have prolonged her life very far.

As for Bolland himself, he said he had always done his best
by her.

In summing up, the coroner said that Dr Statter's evidence
made it clear that Sarah had died from natural causes. He
allowed that there were some 'disgraceful circumstances' but
they were not the province of the inquest. The verdict was that
death had occurred 'by the visitation of God'. There was
criticism of her husband but he was now – in more than one
sense – a free man.

CHAPTER 7

Death After a 'Fair' Fight
1840

Witnesses at the inquest into the death of George Sowerby emphasised that the fight in which he received a fatal blow had been a fair one. Nonetheless, the inquest jury returned a verdict of manslaughter against his opponent, Thomas Murphy, better known as Lanky Tom.

Sowerby and Murphy were both labourers working for contractor John Bishop on the construction of the Leeds and Manchester Railway across Park Hill, Wakefield. On the morning of Wednesday 22 April each was engaged in filling separate waggons with earth from the excavation for the line. About eleven o'clock there was a sudden fall of earth and the two men had a dispute as to which of them had the right to load the loosened soil. According to John Perry, another labourer living in lodgings at Park Hill, the quarrel turned into a fight when Sowerby pitched into Lanky Tom and kicked him to the ground. They wrestled for a few rounds until Lanky Tom, who had been thrown three times, said that he would fight no more amongst the metal and sleepers. The fight was adjourned as the two men moved to the hill top.

Some fifty workmen gathered to watch. Seconds were appointed. The two men fought, it was said, for some seventy-five minutes. Sowerby was the stronger man and for much of the time had the best of the fight. However, in what proved to be the penultimate round, Sowerby was knocked down and when he got up again, Perry said, he looked different. After one more round Sowerby was placed on his second's knee. He held out his hand to Lanky Tom but he was too weak to take it and fell back.

It quickly became clear that Sowerby was seriously hurt. William Statter, a Wakefield surgeon, was sent for and

The Fox and Grapes, *Stanley Road, where the inquest was held into the death of George Sowerby.* The author

arrived at the scene at about 12.30 pm. Sowerby was insensible with two men behind him propping him in an upright position. He had a severe black eye and was badly bruised about his back and chest but his pulse felt full and strong. Statter bled him then and there, opening a vein in his arm and taking, he told the inquest, about 'three gills' (one and a half pints) of blood. Sowerby was taken to his lodgings where Statter visited him again in the early afternoon. He ordered his hair to be shaved and cold applications put to his head. He sent his assistant to the man a little while later. He returned to say that Sowerby was clearly dying. He passed away about 5 pm.

The inquest was held at the *Fox and Grapes* at Eastmoor. Murphy was not present. Statter reported his findings after conducting a post-mortem examination. He had opened Sowerby's skull, which was 'sound and thick', and found a large clot of blood. Death, he said, had been caused by the rupture of a blood vessel in the brain. Otherwise Sowerby had been a very healthy man. Statter also commented on how black and swollen Sowerby's thighs were. Yet James McKay, one of the contractors, who spoke at the inquest insisted, as Perry had done, that there had been no kicking or other unfair play.

Despite the evidence that Sowerby had begun the fight, the jury gave a verdict of manslaughter against Thomas Murphy. But he was nowhere to be found. It was later reported that he had 'evaded the hands of the police', although it was believed that he, too, had been severely injured. Perhaps he returned to Ireland whence, no doubt like many other labourers on the canals and railways, he had come.

CHAPTER 8

The Danger of Accepting a Lift from a Stranger
1844

Girls and young women are regularly warned today of the folly of accepting a lift in a stranger's car. Had Ann Lockwood been told in the 1840s that she must not get into a cart driven by a young man she did not know? Her evidence before the West Riding magistrates at Quarter Sessions suggests that she was, at least, wary.

It was on the afternoon of Thursday, 25 January 1844 that Ann accepted the invitation of one John Whitaker to have a lift. Ann, an out-of-work servant, was walking home to Wakefield from Dewsbury. Whitaker was returning with the horse and cart to Hallilay's dye works in Chald Lane. Ann said that she accepted the lift only because it was raining and that she sat on the rail on one side of the cart and Whitaker sat on the other. Whitaker stopped en route at the *Cross Keys* public house. He brought a glass out to the cart and tried to persuade Ann to have a drink. She refused, no doubt fearing that she might become less alert. Under pressure, she eventually put the glass to her lips but did not even taste the liquor.

A little way up Chald Lane Ann got down from the cart to make the rest of her way home. She asked Whitaker if he would take anything for the lift but he said he would not. Ann had intended to make her way up Westgate and then down Kirkgate to her parents' home at Primrose Hill but Whitaker told her that it would be quicker to cross the field to the 'new road' past Fawcett's mill. This was the Ings Road turnpike. In the dark she missed her way and got onto Smithson's waggon way, the colliery railway running from Low Laithes to the River Calder at Thornes Lane. She turned back and found herself confronted by Whitaker. He threw her to the ground.

She struggled to get up again but as fast as she tried to rise, Whitaker pushed her down again. His clothes were 'disordered' and he tried to pull her clothes up. She screamed as loudly as she could. Whitaker put one hand across her mouth and with the other tried again to get her clothes up. She in turn tried to keep her skirts down.

Ann's screams had been heard by John Calverley from the bottom of Garden Street. He ran down the field towards Law Hill and then turned down the waggon way, asking Whitaker what he thought he was doing. Whitaker claimed that he was doing 'now't' and walked away. Calverley asked Ann who she was but she answered that she would rather not tell and that she would prefer to 'sit down with the injury' than to be exposed in court. Her reaction is not uncommon amongst rape victims today.

Calverley walked with Ann as far as the gate at the bottom of Garden Street and then summoned a boy, George Ralph, to accompany her to her home. At first Ann said nothing about the incident to her parents but the next day she told them what had happened. The following day she reported the incident to the magistrates' clerk.

So it was that on 4 February Whitaker appeared before the court charged with committing an assault with intent to commit rape.

Whitaker's barrister tried to defend his client by implying that Ann was a willing partner and by no means as respectable as she appeared – the perennial defence of someone charged with rape. Had she not allowed the young man to sit close to her in the cart as he held an umbrella over her? Had she not sat on his knee? Ann firmly denied the allegations. She insisted that as she and George reached the Ings bar, Whitaker had come up to them and apologised for assaulting her. He had told her that he 'deserved to be horse-whipped for what he had done' and asked if they could 'make it up'. She said that she 'sent him about his business'. The defending counsel asked her whether this was really true, aiming again to cast doubt in the minds of the jurors.

Happily for Ann there was a witness to the encounter at the bar. Young George Ralph gave the court a clear account of how

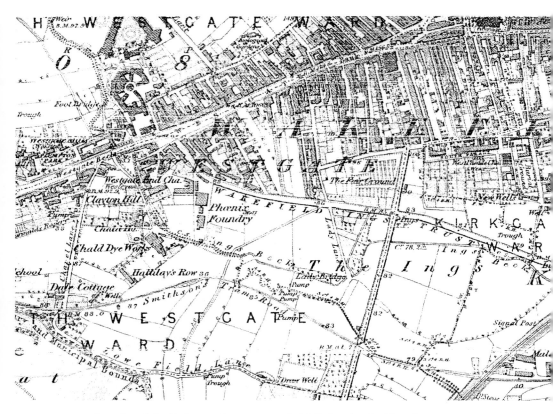

A section of the Ordnance Survey map of c1850 showing Smithson's waggon way, which Ann Lockwood took by mistake, and Ings Road.

Whitaker had come up to them, told the girl he was 'very sorry' for what he had done and said – as Ann had claimed – that he 'deserved to be horse-whipped'.

The jurors found Whitaker guilty of 'high assault' and the magistrates sentenced him to two months' imprisonment.

CHAPTER 9

The Victim was the Constable
1849

The only people who suffered ultimately when Edward Craven buried his illegitimate daughter's baby were the assistant constable who witnessed the post-mortem and his family.

Edward Craven, a retired tradesman in his late fifties who had been born in Bradford, was still a comparative newcomer to Horbury in 1849. He had had a house built there for himself in Lydgate some seven or eight years previously and had brought a young woman to live with him who was initially known as Emma Lister but then introduced as his daughter, Miss Craven. In fact, some of the Horbury residents suspected that she was really his mistress. The Craven household included a servant, who seems to have been a maid of all work, Ellen Sykes. One Thomas Nettleton, described in some reports as a butcher, did occasional work for Mr Craven as a manservant and gardener.

For some time a young man from Huddersfield, also named Lister, was a frequent visitor at Craven's house, often stopping there overnight but at the time of the inquest into the dead baby, he was said to have gone away to Australia.

In the first half of 1849 it was apparent to Ellen Sykes that Miss Craven was pregnant. On Saturday 4 August she seemed poorly and took to her bed. Her father attended her himself, refusing to call a doctor and barring Ellen from the room. It seems that Thomas Nettleton also had strong suspicions for he pressed Ellen the next day for news of the young woman.

On 6 August Ellen saw Mr Craven digging a hole in the garden. That afternoon she was sent out on an errand. When she came back, Miss Craven had ventured downstairs and it was clear to the servant that, if she had been pregnant, she was so no longer. The hole had been filled in.

Lydgate House, Horbury, where Edward Craven buried the still-born baby in the shrubbery. The author

On both 6 and 7 August, Nettleton raised the question of Miss Craven's health with Ellen, remarking that he had heard people say that they 'knew what was the matter with her'. Then, on the Wednesday morning, Nettleton came to Craven's cow house, where Ellen was doing the milking, and showed her a bundle. Inside the brown paper wrapping was a layer of calico, and inside that was a baby boy, quite dead. He had, he said, dug the body up from Craven's garden. Nettleton reburied the body but news of the incident got about and in the small hours of Friday morning the assistant constable, Joseph Berry, with the township constable Roger Hirst and another assistant, John Gee, called at Nettleton's house. He agreed to bring the baby to them at the *Fleece Inn* later in the morning. There Joseph Berry took charge of it and took it to his home.

Berry then went to Wakefield to see the coroner, Thomas Lee. While in Wakefield he heard that Craven and his daughter had absconded and that he was being blamed for not arresting them earlier. He went to the station to check whether they had left by train and then returned to Horbury to watch the local surgeon, George Greenwood, conduct a post-mortem examination.

Then Berry learned that Edward Craven had returned to his house, alone, and there he arrested him leaving him there under the supervision of another constable, George Rayner. But Craven gave Rayner the slip and again disappeared. Berry felt certain that he would be blamed and even feared that he would be imprisoned for allowing a supposed murderer to escape. The poor man spent the night of Friday 10 August searching for Craven, going to all the railway stations in the area as far as Oakenshaw Station. And then he attended the inquest at the *Fleece* in Horbury looking pale and drawn.

At the inquest evidence was given by both Ellen Sykes and Thomas Nettleton, as well as by the surgeon, Greenwood, who gave his view that the baby had been five or six weeks premature and had been still-born.

The solicitor who had attended the inquest on behalf of the authorities, a Mr Stringer, went to Wakefield the following Monday to obtain a warrant from the magistrates for the arrest of Craven and Emma and, but only after they had re-examined Ellen Sykes, Thomas Nettleton and George Greenwood, this was issued.

It was not until 9 September that Craven came before the West Riding magistrates. The charge was simply that of concealing a birth. Ellen Sykes gave evidence that Miss Craven had been pregnant and that the pregnancy had come to an end during that August weekend. Craven was committed for trial at York Assizes but was granted bail.

The hunt was still on for Emma Craven. In mid October news came from the chief police officer at Keighley that someone who might well be the missing woman was to be found in Colne. He asked that someone go over there to identify her and on 11 October she was arrested. She was kept over the weekend in the charge of Ann Kennedy, wife of Colne's sergeant of police, and then brought before Colne magistrates the following Monday. They could find no grounds for pursuing any charges against her and she was released. However, Mrs Kennedy then reported what Emma had told her during her weekend's stay – that she had certainly had a baby and that it was the child of her cousin who had gone to Australia. Emma was re-arrested and was committed for trial along with her father at York.

At the Assizes the prosecuting barrister, a Mr Blanshard, admitted that he really did not see that there was any case to answer. Father and daughter were acquitted.

But the assistant constable, Joseph Berry, was dead. After all his exertions and anxiety in August, he had become deranged. He tried to kill himself and was taken into care at an asylum in York where he died on 27 August. He left a widow and six children.

The 1851 census shows Edward Craven still living in Horbury when he was described as a land proprietor. The only other person resident at Lydgate House then was a twenty-two year old servant, Elizabeth Shaw.

CHAPTER 10

Death of a Horbury Carpenter on the High Seas 1851

Perhaps it was an acquaintance with Captain Lawson when he lived in Horbury that led carpenter Jeremiah Martin, himself a native of Horbury, to enlist under the command of the Captain when he sailed in the *Herald* from Leith to San Francisco in 1850. He met his death, with Lawson and the Captain's wife, at the hands of mutineers the following year. Martin may have been one of the family of Martins who were boatbuilders at Horbury Bridge. Lawson himself was a native of Scarborough but had a house in Horbury.

The *Herald* was built at Sunderland in 1850 for the Halifax firm of Haigh, stone merchants. It was registered in Leith and first sailed from Sunderland with a cargo of coal for San Francisco. Here, Captain Lawson fell sick with cholera and might well have died had it not been for the devoted attention of his wife. All but one of his crew left the ship to prospect for gold. Martin remained, fatally, with the ship. Lawson mustered an American crew and the *Herald* went on to China, trading along the coast there. Then, on 26 August 1851, the ship left Shanghai with a cargo of tea and silk to return to Britain. This time Lawson manned the ship with the only crew to be had, two European mates, a steward, a Portugese seaman and a group of twelve Phillipinos from Manila.

Trouble came from the Manila men. Once out to sea, Lawson issued the daily supply of food and drink. The Phillipinos were not prepared to accept what they saw as a very sparing allowance of the latter. Over and again they demanded more. Every time, Lawson refused. The twelve then determined to kill Lawson and the other Europeans. They drew the Portugese seaman into their confidence. He offered to poison the officers but deliberately slipped so little into their coffee that, although they were made sick, they all survived. This seems to have been a ploy on the Portugese's part for he found an opportunity to tell Lawson of the plot. Lawson warned his officers to stay armed at all times and to have a muster of the Phillipinos each evening and to remove any knives in their possession.

The precautions served to delay the mutiny only for a few days. On the twenty-fifth night of the voyage, the Portugese seaman was, he claimed, called onto the deck to be told by one of the Manila men that the captain and the officers were now 'in the next world' and that the Phillipinos were in charge of the ship. The seaman was ordered to assist in getting the bodies overboard. Weights were tied to the dead captain, the mates and the carpenter, Jeremiah Martin, and they were thrown into the sea. For the time Mrs Lawson, the cook, the steward and the Portugese were spared. However, five days later there was more slaughter. The steward, the cook, and now the Portugese too, were tied up. When the steward begged for mercy, one of the Phillipinos split his head with a hatchet and ripped his body with a knife. However, the cook and the Portugese were set free again.

Now the mutineers decided to scuttle the ship. They loaded everything of value that they could into one of the boats and prepared to leave it. They had not brought themselves to kill Mrs Lawson but they now locked her in a cabin and left her to drown as the ship went down.

The mutineers, still with the Portugese and the cook amongst them, came ashore at Sjilankang, Java. Here, seeing the loot that they carried and perhaps because there were no officers amongst them, the Dutch Resident became suspicious of their story that they had been in a Spanish vessel which had foundered. They were all arrested and sent to Singapore to await trial.

Mutiny and murder would seem to have been by no means uncommon where merchant ships were concerned in this period and the same report – months later than the events themselves – in *The Times* of the tragedy on board the *Herald* referred also to the massacre on 10 December 1851 of the crew of another British ship, the *Victory*, commanded by William Lennox Mullens, which was transporting some 300 Coolies in the China seas. The Coolies seized the ship's ammunition and killed all but one of the crew, sparing one to take the helm and bring them to land.

CHAPTER 11

Rape on a Turnpike
1852

Jane Stakes was immensely brave to give clear and straightforward evidence to West Riding magistrates after she had been raped on 30 June 1852. In fact, her account of her ordeal was sufficiently graphic for the local newspaper to censor it. But it led to the conviction of her assailants.

Jane was a mere fifteen. The attack happened in broad daylight on a public highway, the Wakefield-Doncaster road which, in those days, was a toll road, or turnpike. Jane, who lived in Sharlston, was on her way to Wakefield when, at Oakenshaw, she saw three young men coming towards her. She stepped into the road to avoid contact with them. However, although two of the youths continued past her, the third one stopped. He was twenty-three year old Isaac Marsden. 'I'll cuddle thee,' he anounced, but it was rather more than a cuddle that he had in mind. He threw Jane into the ditch at the side of the road. She screamed and resisted his attack. He then said, 'If thee doesna' hold thy tongue, I'll stick thee'. While he violated her, his two comrades, Solomon and Richard Tankard, in their early twenties, looked on ready to give Marsden warning if anyone approached. No one did.

When he had 'had his way with her', as the report put it, Marsden searched for her money, putting his hand in her pocket and then down her cleavage. Finally, he peeled off her gloves, finding two half-crowns and three penny pieces in one of them, wrapped in a paper. He selected half a crown and threw the gloves and the remaining coins down.

When the three men were safely on their way, Jane set out again for Wakefield. At the bridge over the railway, she met William Grace, a scythe-stone cutter. Grace saw that she was dishevelled and realised that she was upset. She told him that a man had 'done what he liked' with her and robbed her of the half crown. Grace sent Robert Leek and two other men in pursuit of the lads whilst he fetched the township constable, Richard Collingworth.

Leek and his assistants caught up with Marsden and the two Tankards near the *Masons Arms* (where the *Royal Oak* is in Crofton today) where they detained them. They ordered some beer for which Marsden paid with the half-crown. Leek took it up to show to the police. Jane was taken to Crofton to identify them. When she reached home she told her invalid mother about the incident and that evening told her father too.

At the hearing before the magistrates, Jane's father, Jesse Stakes, said that he thought this trouble would be too much for his sick wife.

The three men were all committed for trial at York Assizes on a charge of rape. There, the charge was changed by the Grand Jury to one of 'Felonious assault' (see introduction). The case was heard on 23 July. None of the men offered any defence and, although only Marsden had committed the act, all three were found guilty. Marsden was sentenced to twenty years' transportation and the Tankards each to twelve years' transportation. One wonders whether the possibility of a new life in Australia actually persuaded them not to defend themselves.

CHAPTER 12

The Murder Victim's Body was Exhibited for a Fee
1853

New Street, Wakefield, had a bad reputation in Victorian times as *Foul Deeds and Suspicious Deaths in Wakefield* (2001) reveals. But rarely can it have seen so macabre an episode as the exhibition one weekend in 1853 of a murdered girl to paying sightseers.

The body was that of nineteen-year old Catherine, or Kitty, Sheridan. She had been killed by her former lover, Henry Dobson.

Kitty Sheridan had had a wretched life. She had been born in Doncaster, one of six children. Her mother had died when she was eight and her father had absconded, leaving his family to the

Jacob's Well Lane where Henry Dobson was arrested. The author

mercies of relatives and the workhouse. At fourteen Kitty had gone into service but had been seduced and compelled to leave. Like many another girl in a similar situation, she had become a prostitute. In 1850 or 1851 she went to live with Ann Clough, another young woman of easy virtue and ruined reputation, in a modest, one-up-one-down dwelling in a yard off New Street.

Henry Dobson was a thirty-year old widower when he met Kitty some time late in 1852. A handsome man, earning good money as a joiner and cabinet-maker, he soon persuaded the girl to go to live with him. He was described as of slender frame and below middle stature, with small, regular features, light brown hair and a fair complexion. But Henry enjoyed a drink and once he was inebriated he treated Kitty so violently that she returned to Ann Clough's and on 11 February, 1853 brought a charge against him for assault. The magistrates bound him over to keep the peace but he swore to Constable George Gibson, who had arrested him, that he would 'take her life' for what she had done.

On the evening of Friday 18 February Ann and Kitty went to the *Carriers Arms* for a drink. Dobson was there. He glowered at Kitty so viciously that the two young women swiftly left. Some time after ten o'clock that evening they went to a shop in New Street to buy their supper – bacon and a loaf of bread. Back at the hovel where they lived, Ann remembered that they had meant to buy cheese. She left Kitty frying the bacon, with only the light from a low fire, whilst she went back to the shop. Fatally, she left the door unlocked.

It was ten past eleven when Ann returned. There was an ominous stillness in the house. As Ann's eyes adjusted to the darkness she saw Kitty lying on the floor. A neighbour, Thomas Burkinshaw, brought a lamp. Kitty's throat had been slit from ear to ear. She was already dead. A bloodstained razor lay nearby. Burkinshaw summoned the police and Dr William Swift Wade.

There was never any doubt that Henry Dobson had committed the vile deed. Thomas Towler, a lamplighter, said that he had seen Dobson coming out of the yard where the girls lived just after 11pm. A few minutes later he was seen running down Kirkgate by Harriet Wolfinden. He shouted to her, 'Oh, Harriet, I've done the job, I've killed Kitty'. Dobson

St John's churchyard where Kitty Sheridan was buried. Wakefield Historical Publications.

was arrested by Constable Stringer in Jacob's Well Lane shortly before 2 am on Saturday 19 February. He offered no resistance and readily admitted to the killing. His coat and left hand were caked with blood.

The inquest was held that Saturday evening at the *Albion Inn* in Westmorland Street. The jury brought a verdict of wilful murder against Henry Dobson.

Meanwhile, Ann Clough was making the most of the misfortune! Kitty's body was laid out in her upstairs room and Ann collected payment from the many people who braved the unsavoury yard on Saturday and Sunday to see it.

Kitty was buried the following Tuesday in St John's churchyard. The chief mourners were a brother and sister from Doncaster. A number of 'women of the night', neatly dressed in black, were present.

Dobson was tried at the Spring Assizes in York in March. His defending counsel made a plea for a verdict of manslaughter rather than murder. Dobson had gone to the house hoping to persuade Kitty to return to him, he said. The murder was not premeditated. But Dobson had taken the razor with him to the house. He was found guilty of murder and sentenced to death.

In the three weeks before he was hung, a group of Wakefield people got up a petition seeking to have the sentence commuted. It was taken by Wakefield MP George Sanders to the Home Secretary. But it was to no avail.

However, before his execution, Dobson earned the reputation of being a model prisoner. He spent time reading and praying with the chaplain at York Castle, Reverend Thomas Sutton, and he wrote letters to friends in Wakefield expressing his remorse and asking for an account of Kitty's funeral.

Dobson was executed at mid-day on Saturday 9 April at York Castle. In the morning Sutton gave him the sacrament. He walked with a firm step to the scaffold and prayed again for a few moments with Sutton before his death. A crowd of 'less than five thousand' watched the spectacle.

The *Wakefield Express*, which in those days came out on Saturdays, published a late edition the same day to give an account of his final moments.

CHAPTER 13

Found Drowned
1860

How could a man who was healthy and sober drown in the few inches of water in the Ings Beck?

That was the question that faced an inquest jury at *The Graziers Arms*, George Street, Wakefield in January 1860. Their deliberations were the more difficult since they had no idea who the man was or what he was doing in Wakefield on the day that he died.

The body was seen in the water at about three in the afternoon of Thursday 5 January by a local lad. It was lying face downwards but the water was so shallow that the man's back was uncovered. It was in a stretch of the beck quite close to where the railway crosses Denby Dale Road. The police were summoned and, as was customary for centuries, it was taken to a nearby public house, in this case *The Graziers*, to await the coroner.

The man was stoutly built, about 5′6″ in height, and wore a pilot-cloth jacket and cord trousers which were somewhat scorched as though he had worked at a furnace. There was a red spotted silk handkerchief about his neck. He had three shillings and sixpence in his pocket and a tobacco box. Dr Walker, who conducted a post-mortem examination, said he could find no trace of intoxicants in the body.

Could he have been murdered? There was a wound on his temple but this could have been caused by a fall rather than a blow. And seemingly robbery was not a motive.

A local policeman said that he had seen the man in the early hours of Thursday morning walking from Westgate into Ings Road. He walked alone and there was no one else about.

The inquest jury brought in a verdict simply of 'found drowned'. A photograph was taken of the dead man and

The Graziers Arms, *George Street where the body later identified as that of Abraham Rhodes was taken.* The author

circulated widely. This must, surely, have been a very early instance of photography being used in detective work.

The unknown man was then buried in Wakefield cemetery.

The following Tuesday, Richard Rhodes, a blacksmith, of Cutler Heights, Tong, came forward to identify the man as his brother, Abraham. Some years earlier Abraham had worked in Wakefield for Messrs Woodhead, Patchett and Hunter, colliery owners, of Westgate Common. More recently he had been working and lodging with his brother. However, at Christmas he had said that he would like to see some of his old friends in Wakefield.

On Wednesday 4 January Abraham had set out for Wakefield, presumably walking all the way. But no one came forward to say that he had visited them and how he met his death was never discovered.

CHAPTER 14

So Who Did Kill Elizabeth Mitchell?
1860

When the case came before York Assizes in December 1860, seventeen-year old George Thorpe was acquitted of the charge of murdering his fellow farm servant, fourteen year old Elizabeth Mitchell. So who did kill her? Granted there was no obvious motive for the murder, Thorpe seems to have been the only person with any opportunity to shoot her.

Thorpe and Elizabeth were employed by Thomas Spink, the tenant of Upton Farm which he had leased from J M Hepworth a year or so before the murder. The modest farmhouse was close to the Wakefield-Askern road. Downstairs it had two living rooms and a kitchen; there were three bedrooms upstairs. The back door opened into the kitchen and immediately outside it was an outhouse used for coal. There were a number of labourers' cottages quite close by. The village of Upton was small with a population of only 180–200.

Thorpe, described as a sullen and morose character, had come from Fenwick, near Askern in March 1860 to work as a farm hand for Mr Spink. Elizabeth had been with the Spinks since November 1859. Her family lived at North Elmsall within easy walking distance of Upton.

Elizabeth was murdered on Sunday afternoon, 2 September 1860. Mr and Mrs Spink, who had only recently been married, had gone out to visit friends in Darrington and the girl had been left in charge of the house. Mrs Spink had left supplies of tea, sugar, bread and cheese for the servants' evening meal with a bottle of beer for Thorpe. A friend, sixteen-year old Annie Cookson, who lived nearby, joined Elizabeth for a time as did Elizabeth's sister, Martha. Thorpe spent the earlier part of the afternoon with another farm-hand, Robert Rhodes, and 'Mr Burkett's lad' at the Upton premises of shopkeeper Mary Waller where they shared three bottles of ginger beer. He left his friends at 3.40 pm saying that he must 'fetch the beasts' but arranged to meet Rhodes again in the early evening to go to Walton Wood. He returned to the farmhouse while the three girls were together. There was a certain amount of joking and skylarking as one might expect when young people are unsupervised. Thorpe tried to take Annie's headband from her, and Elizabeth pulled Thorpe's hair. Annie said at the inquest that the lad then used some threatening language.

Annie left at about five o'clock to go home for her tea. Martha set out for home at the same time, leaving Thorpe and Elizabeth alone. Annie returned at six to find the front door of the farmhouse locked. There was no one about. She thought Elizabeth must be at work milking the cows but she was not in the cowhouse. It was when she approached the back door that Annie found her friend lying dead in the coal store. Who could have done it except Thorpe?

Annie cried for help, screaming 'Elizabeth's laid in the coal hole', and her father, William Cookson, and another neighbour, Joseph Thorpe, came running. The two men carried the dead girl into the kitchen. The underside of her clothing was saturated with blood. She had been shot in the left side close to the spine and just under the shoulder blade.

George Thorpe returned shortly afterwards having been to meet Robert Rhodes as he had arranged although Rhodes said at the inquest that he had been late for the appointment and he had had to go and look for him. He saw him at five past six running up the road from the direction of the farm. Cookson chided George for not staying with Elizabeth and guarding the farmhouse. Thorpe remarked, 'Well, this is a damned queer thing', and then repeated twice, 'I have not done it. I have not done it.' Cookson's response was, 'I never said you had'. Thorpe told Annie that he had left Elizabeth at the farmhouse alive and well and with both back and front doors bolted and had gone up Cook Close to look after the sheep.

Thorpe was sent to Darrington to summon the Spinks home. Dr James Ibeson was sent for from Hemsworth and

Constable Joseph Skelton was called in from South Elmsall. Mr and Mrs Spink reached the farm about 8pm. Thorpe coolly unharnessed the horse from the gig and then followed them into the house. The policeman remained at the farm all night with Thorpe under surveillance. The following day Police Superintendent Hall came from Pontefract. He examined a gun belonging to Mr Spink which was in the living room next to the kitchen. The farmer said that he kept it for scaring the crows but had not used it for at least month. Hall found, however, that it been recently fired. He asked Thorpe to show him the clothes he had been wearing the previous day. He went with the lad to his bedroom where Thorpe took a blue smock out of his trunk. Hall then arrested Thorpe on a charge of murder and took him to the lock-up in Pontefract. His father, described as a respectable and hard-working man, visited him there that evening and was said to have been 'almost heartbroken'.

Inquiries quickly revealed that Thorpe had been wearing a white smock, not the blue one, when Rhodes saw him. Hall took his prisoner back to the farm and made him open his

South Kirkby church where the funeral of Elizabeth Mitchell was held. The author

trunk again. There was the white smock, and there was blood in a cuff and on the waistband.

The inquest into Elizabeth's death was held at an Upton shop (the village had no public house) on Wednesday 5 September. Thorpe was brought to the hearing but said nothing and maintained a sullen and impassive demeanour. Evidence was given by Dr Ibeson and Dr Clark, from Ackworth, who had examined Elizabeth's body together. It was suggested that the girl had tried to get away from Thorpe and that he had shot her in the back as she was going out of the kitchen door.

Further evidence came from Dr John Lister of Doncaster who had cut open Elizabeth's body and found fourteen pieces of shot embedded in her heart. The shot matched the ammunition kept by Mr Spink. Lister could not say whether the girl, who was 'well-developed' and about 5′3″ tall, had been 'ravished' or not but he was clear that she could not have shot herself.

There was some dissent among the inquest jurors but the majority verdict was that Elizabeth had been murdered by Thorpe. As the inquest concluded, the cortege taking Elizabeth's body to her funeral at South Kirkby passed outside the shop.

Thorpe was brought before West Riding magistrates at the *White Hart Inn*, North Elmsall, on Thursday 6 September. Little new emerged but witnesses agreed that there had been no hostility between Thorpe and Elizabeth. But neither was there any suggestion that anyone else had either motive or opportunity to kill the girl. Thorpe was committed for trial at York Assizes on a charge of murder.

There, Thorpe was, perhaps, lucky. In the days before forensic evidence in regard to fingerprints or blood, the only evidence against him was circumstantial. It was not enough to convict him.

CHAPTER 15

A Tussle over a Newspaper
1861

Technically, Ann Walker died because her son pushed her over. But, in a somewhat chauvinstic summing up of the evidence at the inquest, on 17 January 1861, the coroner said that, while 'morally' William had been the cause of her death, the jury must have nothing to do with that: Ann had taken the consequences of interfering with a drunken man so it was really all her fault.

Ann, who was eighty-one at the time of her death and the widow of a dyer, lived in a cottage at Thornes. Her son lived with her. On the evening of 5 January, she and William had been seated either side of a good fire when their neighbour, Thomas Radcliffe, called to exchange newspapers. William had the paper in his hands at the time but was the worse for drink and it was getting crumpled up. It seems that Ann feared either that he would tear it or that he would get it too near the fire. No doubt she would have felt ashamed to hand it the neighbour in a damaged condition.

Ann asked William to give her the paper. Since he did not respond, she said she would take it from him. She got up and took hold of it. William pulled it out of her hand and said, 'Mother, go sit ye down. I can manage very well,' whereupon he gave her a push. There was an untidy piece of hessian on the floor, in use as a hearthrug. Ann's foot became entangled in this and she lost her balance, falling heavily against the top bar of the fire grate. Radcliffe swiftly caught her up, before she could get burned, and settled her back in her chair. She complained of severe pain in her side and Radcliffe then laid her on the sofa.

Both Radcliffe and his wife, Jane, who looked in on Ann later the same evening, were well aware that the inquest jury might find William guilty of manslaughter. In their evidence they were at pains to emphasise that the fall was an accident. Radcliffe said that William was not in a bad temper and the push had been only a 'little' one. There had been no struggle. The rug was in such a state that anyone could have fallen. Moreover, William was immediately sorry for what had happened. Ann had never blamed her son for her injuries.

Jane Radcliffe told the inquest that Ann had complained to her in previous days of a pain in the head and of giddiness; she had said that a feather would be enough to knock her down. The sacking was a very old piece and had almost caused her husband to trip. Jane herself had taken it up after the fall and thrown it away.

Further evidence was given at the inquest by Samuel Secker, the surgeon who attended Ann in her last days. He had been called in on 9 January. Ann was in bed and he had diagnosed fractured ribs and pleurisy. She also had a chronic cough. He thought that she was in a dangerous state and warned her attendants of this. He visited Ann daily and saw William twice. William had asked him to 'bestow all possible attention' on his mother. Ann was always cheerful when Secker visited her. She was a wonderfully healthy woman for her age and in no way imbecilic or childish and, importantly, she had never blamed William for her injuries.

In his address to the jury, the coroner said that the real cause of death lay in Ann's getting up to take the paper from her son. He had stopped her getting the paper, but he had a perfect right to do that.

The jury's verdict was one of 'accidental death'.

CHAPTER 16

He Would Not Take No
For An Answer
1861

Stonemason Thomas Scott had an unblemished reputation until he met Caroline Furniss in 1861. He had worked for 'Prophet' Wroe at Melbourne House, Wrenthorpe, for some twenty years. Now a widower of fifty, he met thirty-year old Caroline at Whitsuntide. Caroline, who was living in Kirkgate, was married but had lived apart from her husband for eleven years. She claimed to earn her living by dressmaking and millinery but admitted that she did sometimes 'cohabit' although only with one man at a time.

Kirkgate in the 1880s. Here Thomas Scott shot Caroline Furniss at Clarkson's eating house. Wakefield Historical Publications.

No doubt Scott wanted a companion and someone to keep his house. Perhaps, too, he was physically attracted to the young woman. Caroline went to Scott's house in Snow Hill for some weeks 'to clean' for him. Whether she lodged there or whether she provided other comforts is unclear. But, unaware of her married state, Scott pressed her to marry him and when she refused the relationship turned sour.

Caroline took lodgings in Warrengate. In early July 1861, Scott came to the house to seek her out. She saw the outline of a pistol in his pocket and she saw him put his hand to it. She seized his coat and rushed for the door. She then ran out of the house and did not return until the following day. She made a complaint to the police. Scott came back a day later to her lodgings but she kept the door bolted. It was, she decided, time for her to move on. She sold her few possessions and went to York.

However, on 26 July, Caroline went back to Wakefield, intending to make just a short visit. She went to the *Spotted Leopard* in Kirkgate and there – although she claimed there had been no appointment – she met Scott again. He took her for a meal to the nearby Clarkson's eating house where she took a room for the night. He called on her the next day and the day after that. She told him that she must now return to York. He suggested they go for a walk together and, as she was tying on her bonnet, he put a pistol against her side and fired it. Only her whalebone stays prevented her from injury. Somehow she got away from him and fled down the stairs where Charles Clarkson fastened her in the kitchen for her own safety. Two of Clarkson's customers, Levi Beaumont and Richard Tempest, seized Scott and held him until the police arrived. They saw Scott attempt to hide his pistol in the fireplace but prevented him from doing so. Inspector Frost took Caroline's shawl, belt and jacket, all marked with gunshot and smelling of gunpowder, as evidence. Constable Frost took the gun and was able to confirm that it had been fired very recently.

Scott was brought before the magistrates where his solicitor claimed that he was a man of exemplary character and tried to show that Caroline was 'asking for it'. He pointed out that she had lived formerly in Thackray's Yard, off Kirkgate, and that that was not at all a respectable address.

Nonetheless, Scott was committed for trial at York Assizes. The case was heard at the Winter Gaol Delivery on 13 December. Scott claimed that the pistol had gone off by accident. However, the jury found him guilty and he was sentenced to seven years penal servitude.

CHAPTER 17

A Murderous Attack on the Barnsley Canal
1872

Ralph Greenwood must have had a remarkably strong constitution. Not only did he walk some distance along the Barnsley Canal bleeding profusely and with a fractured skull, but he actually prepared the next lock for his boat to go through before going to the lock-keeper's house and then on to the home of the local policeman.

Greenwood, whose home was in Netherton, was a powerfully-built man and the skipper of an open boat, the *Grecian Bend*, belonging to the Oaks Colliery Company. He had spent the night of Tuesday, 27 August 1872 at home with his wife (the couple had twelve children), leaving the laden boat in charge of

A coal boat on the Barnsley Canal near the bridge on the lane to Walton Hall. The John Goodchild Collection.

his eighteen year old son, Joseph, who usually worked with the horse, and another hand, Thomas Dixon. Leaving home at 6 am, Greenwood took the train to Walton and then walked up the towpath to rejoin the boat at Cold Hiendley, just below the reservoir, to bring it down to the Aire and Calder Navigation at Wakefield on their way to Sowerby Bridge.

A slower vessel, owned by William Fieldhouse and with a nine-inch greater draught than the *Grecian Bend*, was ahead of them as Greenwood's boat reached the bridge near Walton Hall. It was about 9 am. Just before the canal narrowed for the bridge there was a reasonable place to pass and Greenwood called to its skipper, Sam Mountain, to let him get by. There was a dispute. Greenwood drew the *Grecian Bend* alongside Mountain's and stepped onto it. A woman, described as 'living with' Mountain, but later named as his wife, Emma, was cutting cabbages with a knife. She rushed at the intruder with this but his fustian waistcoat warded off the blow. Mountain then seized a small hatchet and attacked Greenwood with it, dealing a number of blows to his head until the handle flew off and the deck of his barge was spattered with blood. There was a deep wound to the forehead where the bone had been shattered. His sealskin cap, cut through in several places and drenched with blood, fell off and was retrieved by his son.

For a few moments, Greenwood lay insensible amid the coals. Then he got up to go ashore. Mountain seized him round the neck and tried to choke him. But Greenwood got away and staggered down to towpath, filling the next lock ready for his boat as he went. He called at the lock house, still bleeding profusely, had a cup of tea with the keeper, Robert Hardisty, and, when his boat arrived, changed his waistcoat and hat before making his way to the police house. Constable Newton arrested Sam and Emma Mountain. Greenwood was taken to Dr Horsfall's surgery and then to Clayton Hospital. The two prisoners were brought before West Riding magistrates later the same day and remanded in custody. At a court hearing on 7 September both were charged with maliciously wounding Ralph Greenwood. Emma was given bail.

That day it became clear that Greenwood's condition was worsening. Percy Tew JP went with Superintendent Hall to see

The top lock and lock-house on the Barnsley Canal at Walton. The John Goodchild Collection.

him at the hospital and, in the presence of the house surgeon, Hugh Warriner, they heard his evidence. He died the following evening at 9.45 pm.

The inquest was held at the *Royal Hotel* in Wood Street the following day. Warriner, who had carried out a post-mortem examination, said that four of the axe-wounds had been only superficial but the fifth had fractured Greenwood's skull. He had found an abscess under the wound about the size of a hen's egg. Whilst Greenwood was in his care, he had

work some time between 3 am and 4 am carrying a lamp to guide them in the darkness and fog.

Furbisher, who was dead drunk according to the miners, stopped them, asked who they were and asked them to take him to his house which was, he is alleged to have said, at Warmfield. He promised them each a good day's wages. The miners agreed to the bargain.

Slowly the odd trio made their way to Warmfield, Furbisher staggering and stumbling along and jingling his money in his pocket. At Warmfield he admitted that he really lived in Crofton, near the *Cock*, and required his escorts to take him there. Eventually the group reached Furbisher's house where his aunt acted as his housekeeper and where a servant-girl, Annie Jackson, was roused and let them in.

Furbisher then offered his guides his notion of hospitality – a breakfast of gin and a cigar – and gave them sixpence. Furbisher took off his boots and lounged on the sofa. It is over what followed that the accounts were somewhat 'misty'.

The Hark to Mopsey public house in Normanton in 2003. Here the two miners met Richard Furbisher in the fog. The author

Kerney, it is said, went out to the saddle-room in the yard where one of Furbisher's men was sleeping. Whittingham claimed to have waited in the house because he expected Furbisher 'as a gentleman' to keep to his agreement and give both men a proper wage. He waited in vain and then set out to join Kerney but, or so he claimed, Furbisher followed him and struck him a frightful blow on the top of his head. He thought it must have been with a heavy walking stick. He fell to the ground senseless, bleeding profusely from a head wound. When he came to, he called for Kerney but his fellow miner did not hear him. A Nostell labourer, Joseph Smith, was passing by and he called to another passer-by, Mr Dyson, a painter with a business in Wood Street, Wakefield, who was out looking for one of his workmen. Dyson sent for the village constable, P C William Coombs who organized Whittingham's being taken to the *Royal Oak* public house. Dyson then went back to Wakefield to fetch the police surgeon, Dr John Whiteley. The doctor reached the *Royal Oak* at 10.15 am where he found Whittingham pale and feeble. He dressed his wounds and sent him home to Normanton in a cart belonging to a local farmer named Smith. Once home, Whittingham was put in the care of Dr McKenzie.

Meanwhile, Constable Coombs charged Furbisher with assault and attempted to take him into custody. Furbisher resisted and, according to the constable's evidence at the inquest, threatened him with further violence. Coombs send for P C Agnew who was stationed at Heath to give him assistance but, as Agnew was in Wakefield, Coombs enlisted the aid of another local farmer, a Mr Cullingworth. By the afternoon, Furbisher was in the lock-up in Wakefield.

Two days later, on 15 October, Furbisher was brought before the West Riding magistrates. J C D Charlesworth was in the chair and with him were Dr D B Kendall, S G Leatham and Major Barker. The court was crowded with Wakefield tradespeople and some of Furbisher's Crofton neighbours. The charge was read out: that on 13 October at Crofton Furbisher did maliciously wound and inflict grievous bodily harm on George Whittingham. The magistrates were handed a medical certificate showing that Whittingham was too sick to

The Court House in Wood Street, Wakefield, where crowds gathered to watch the trial of Richard Furbisher. The author

appear. Furbisher's solicitor then asked for bail promising the court that he could prove that his client was fast asleep at the time Whittingham fell down and that his injuries were the result of that fall. Although Coombs told the court how Furbisher had threatened him, bail was granted on the sureties of John Scott, a hatter, and Richard Scowby, a wine and spirit merchant who had a business in Westgate, Wakefield (perhaps he supplied Furbisher with his gin!).

The case was heard ten days later, on 25 October. Crowds came to the court from Ackworth, Barnsley, Horbury and Ossett as well as from Crofton, Heath and Normanton. Whittingham was now at least fit enough to attend the hearing although he was described as looking 'like a corpse risen from the dead'. His head was extensively bandaged and he shook 'like an aspen leaf'. When he gave evidence he was allowed to sit down at the solicitors' table. He said that he, Kerney and Furbisher had reached Furbisher's home at 6.10 am. He agreed that he had drunk some gin but insisted that it had been mixed with water. As he was going out he had seen Furbisher following him with a big stick in his hand. He admitted that he did not see Furbisher strike the blow but insisted that no one else was about and he had undoubtedly been hit. Kerney had come to him in the yard and tried to get help from the house but the door had been shut against them.

Dr Whiteley said that Whittingham had lost between three and four pints of blood but, under cross questioning, he agreed that whilst the wound could have been made by a heavy stick, it could equally have been caused by Whittingham's falling backward and knocking his head on a stone. Moreover, he threw doubt on how serious the miner's injuries really were by suggesting that he did not need to wear quite so many bandages.

Considerably more doubt was soon thrown on the miner's version of events. The Nostell labourer, Joseph Smith, who was likely to have been a critical witness, did not appear. Furbisher's solicitor, Wainwright, stressed how respectable his client was. He admitted that he had been 'in liquor' but emphasised that the miners were too; they had had a 'full fling' at half a gallon of gin. Furbisher had needed their help to get home only because of the fog, not because he was incapably drunk. Once home, Wainwright said, Furbisher had taken his boots off and changed into a pair of slippers in which he certainly could not do much harm. Furbisher had been half asleep in his armchair when Whittingham was supposed to have gone out and the attack had allegedly taken place.

Reading the evidence that Wainwright gathered together, one is struck that every witness he called was in some way financially dependent on Furbisher. A key testifier was Richard Briggs, Furbisher's gardener cum groom. He said he had been called when the three men got back to Crofton to take off Furbisher's boots; the miners were then drinking gin. He had taken the boots out to clean them and when he brought them back Whittingham had left the house with him. They had stood by the coal heap where Briggs had taken out his snuff box. Whittingham had said, 'I'll have a pinch with you,' and, taking one, had reeled round and fallen with his head on the coal-heap wall, striking a stone. Briggs had left him lying there.

Thomas Bradley, a young farm hand, confirmed Briggs' version of events. He had, he said, seen what happened when he went up about 8 am to milk the cows. Then it was the turn of the servant, Annie Jackson. She had fetched up the gin for the miners to drink. After his boots were removed, Furbisher had gone to sleep. He had definitely not gone out between 6.30 am and 10 am. Briggs had come in with the boots while Whittingham was in the kitchen and they had gone out together. No one had come to the door for help and she had not told Furbisher that the miner was lying by the coal heap.

A final witness was William Pearson who lived in Northgate, Wakefield, and worked at maltings belonging to Furbisher. He had called at the Crofton house on the morning the miners were there. Furbisher was fast asleep but he saw two men by the coal heap. One, who was bleeding, said, 'Are you the b… that has taken the blood from me?' In his opinion there was not much blood lost at all.

In the end there was no certainty about what had really occurred. P C Coombs' evidence pointed the finger of guilt clearly at Furbisher. He said that when he attempted to arrest Furbisher, the maltster had sworn that he would 'do for him' as he had done for Whittingham. Otherwise the miners had no one to back their version of events. And then, despite his heavy drinking, Furbisher was of a different – and supposedly more respectable and trustworthy – social class from the miners. The magistrates chose to give him the benefit of the doubt and he was discharged.

CHAPTER 19

In Chancery
1884

John Barratt was so incensed that his brother-in-law had taken a family dispute about property to the Court of Chancery that he set out one Sunday morning, in 1884, threatening murder.

Barratt, then aged sixty-three, was a wool sorter living in Old Library Yard, Northgate, Wakefield, and was described as a well-known public figure and active member of the local Conservative party. His brother-in-law, Charles Oates, was a chemist and druggist with his own business at Longroyd Bridge, Huddersfield.

Oates was the sole trustee of the property left by Barratt's father, another John, and the other beneficiaries, John Barratt's brothers, were happy with his conduct of the matter. Barratt never had been, and in March 1879 he had gone to Oates' shop and launched a savage attack upon him. What finally led to Barratt's horrible resolve was the notice in the Wakefield newspapers on 5 April 1884 that the houses, cottages and fields left by his father were to be put up for auction at the *Bull Hotel* on 18 April. They included two shops with living accommodation in Northgate, thirty-four cottages in Barratt's Yard and Old Library Yard, fields at Newton with beds of coal, clay, marl and blue mineral lying under them, and a field at Bragg Lane End.

Early in the morning of Sunday 6 April, Barratt walked to Horbury and took a train from there to Huddersfield. He was carrying a revolver. At about 10.30 am he accosted his brother-in-law as he was walking to the service at Buxton Road Chapel. He demanded that Oates take the case out of Chancery and pulled out the gun. Oates immediately seized him. His shouts brought Samuel Taylor, a wholesale clothier who lived in Buxton Road, to the scene and he took the gun

WOOD TURNING WORKS,

HART YARD,

LITTLE WESTGATE.

———

)ERSHAW,

R, AND PRACTICAL

TMAKER,

'E EMPORIUM,

'GATE, WAKEFIELD.

' TENNIS.

SHIRTS,
TROUSERS,
HATS,
CLUB DESIGNS
made to order, and
registered.
RACQUET HOLDERS,
2s. 6d. each.

Clubs will find all the
above in great variety and
in excellent quality, at

ERSHAW'S,

GATE, WAKEFIELD.

———

)AL ! COAL !

ER, AND BARNSLEY
)ALS.

Drawing-Room, House,
may now be obtained
rom

K OLDHAM,

NGS, WESTGATE,
EFIELD.

b, 9/6, & 8/6 per Ton.
per Ton extra.
. if required. A Trial is
lly solicited.

———

) N S'

Writing and Copying

K S .

ion, Express Office, Wake-
ll Stationers.

———

' TO HOUSEWIVES,
re heavy, and you are
lighter, send your address

Auctioneers' Office, 17, Southgate, Wakefield.

Sale by Mr. Henry Tinker.

IN THE HIGH COURT OF JUSTICE,
1879 B., No. 141.
CHANCERY DIVISION.
MR. JUSTICE KAY.

IN THE MATTER OF THE ESTATE OF JOHN
BARRATT, Deceased.

OATES v. BARRATT.

PARTICULARS AND CONDITIONS OF
SALE of 2 Freehold SHOPS and 34 COTTAGES,
situate in the Old Library Yard and Barratt's Yard,
Northgate, Wakefield, in the County of York ; and of
5 Freehold FIELDS of LAND, situate at Newton and
at Bragg Lane End, near Wakefield aforesaid, and
certain valuable Beds of COAL, CLAY, MARL, and
BLUE METAL lying under parts of the fields situate
at Newton aforesaid, which will be SOLD BY
AUCTION, in Lots, by Mr. HENRY TINKER (the
person appointed by the Judge to whose Court the
above action is attached), at the BULL HOTEL, in
Wakefield, on FRIDAY, the 18th day of April, 1884, at
Six o'clock in the Evening, subject to the conditions
hereinafter mentioned.

Printed Particulars and Conditions of Sale may be
had gratis of Messrs. Fisher and Preston, Solicitors,
Huddersfield ; of Messrs. Iliffe and Cardale, Soli-
citors, 2, Bedford Row, London, W.C. ; of Messrs.
Barratt and Senior, Solicitors, Wakefield ; of Messrs.
H. B. Clarke and Son, Solicitors, 14, Serjeants' Inn,
Fleet Street, London, E.C. ; of Messrs. Franklin and
Humphreys, Solicitors, Halifax ; of Messrs. Jaques,
Layton, and Jaques, Solicitors, 5, Ely Place, London,
E.C. ; of Mr. Thomas James, Solicitor, Llandovery ;
of Messrs. Roche and Son, Solicitors, 33, Old Jewry,
London, E.C. ; of the Auctioneer ; and at the Place
of Sale.

PARTICULARS.

LOT 1.—All that valuable Plot of BUILDING
LAND, formerly described as an Enclosure, now used
as a GARDEN, situate at Bragg Lane End, in the
Bradford Road, near Wakefield, in the County of
York, containing 1 acre or thereabouts, and now in
the occupation of Mr. George Asquith.

LOT 2.—All those TWO valuable Freehold FIELDS,
adjoining the Leeds and Wakefield Turnpike Road
at Newton, near Wakefield aforesaid, containing
8a. 2r. 15p. or thereabouts, and now in the hands of
the Receiver in this action.

And also all those TWO valuable BEDS of COAL,
commonly called or known by the names of the
"Middleton Bed " and the " Beeston Bed," lying and
being under the said Closes of Land, save and except
such parts thereof as are lying and being under the
portion of land recently added to the rest of the said
fields, and which adjoins the road, and contains an
area of about 500 square yards.

[This Lot includes also all such part or parts as still
remain unworked and ungotten, if any, of all those
3 Mines, Beds, or Seams of COAL and SLACK, commonly called " The Cat Coal," " The Scale Coal," and
"The Stanley Main Coal," and of all that Bed of
CLAY, MARL, BIND, BLUE METAL, or other
Strata, as lie within and under the said Closes of
Land, or any part thereof, save and except such parts
of the said Coal, Clay, &c., as are lying and being
under the before-mentioned 500 square yards of land.

N.B.—One Bed or Seam of Coal, commonly called
" The Haigh Moor Bed " and other the here-
ditaments, liberties, and powers granted by an
Indenture, dated the 1st day of June, 1867, an
abstract of which will be open to inspection,
as stipulated in the conditions of sale, are
excepted from the sale of this lot. The above-
mentioned Bed of Seam of Coal has, since the
date of the said Indenture, been gotten.

LOT 3.—A SHOP and DWELLING-HOUSE, front-
ing Northgate, in Wakefield aforesaid, occupied by
Mr. William Boddy, and 16 COTTAGES, forming the
Old L...

them for Next Tues
being no Sale the fol
the Easter Holidays.
Address, HEPPER

———

J. E
GENERAL AUC

ADVANCES made on

VALUES of every
Stoc

———

19, KIRKG
BURLEY STREE

———

To

FOR SALE, fron
MANURE.—A

J. WIGGLESWO
field, has to DI
VICTORIA.—Apply

A BARGAIN.—W
good condition
Apply to SAMUEL WA

FOR SALE, Two
Singer's, ball b
Apply, J. COOKSON, 2

FOR SALE, a ba
PIANO, in good
for £1 10s.—Apply, 8
manton.

FOR SALE, BAG
2ft. 4in. Slate
round ends, screwed l
and marking board.—
WM. BROWN, Nether

100 VIOLINS FO
DUNHILL'S,
side, and Borough Ma

HARP, second-hand
£15, at J. DUN
Cheapside, and Borou

PIANOFORTES, se
DUNHILL'S, 66, W
and Borough Market I

PIANOFORTE, in
£40 ; for cash £1
Corner of Cheapside, a

PIANOFORTE, in
splendid tone,
DUNHILL'S, 66, West
Borough Market Hall

PIANOFORTE, in
in good condition
66, Westgate, Corner
Market Hall

PIANOFORTE, wal
pass ; cheek act
J. DUNHILL'S, 66, West
Borough Market Hall

PIANOFORTE, gre
to be sold chea
Corner of Cheapside, a

PIANOFORTE, in
full compass ; v
cost £32 a few months a
taken. Call and see th
Southgate, Wakefield

The advertisement in the Wakefield Express *on 5 April 1884 for the sale of properties in the Northgate area of Wakefield which incensed John Barratt.*

from Barratt. Barratt was then taken into custody by a police constable.

The following morning, Barratt was brought before Huddersfield magistrates charged with attempting to shoot with intent to murder. There was evidence of premeditation: a surveyor who had been in Wakefield the previous year to look at the properties reported that Barratt had told him that he intended to shoot Oates. Barratt was committed for trial at Leeds Assizes and taken meanwhile to Wakefield prison.

At his trial in May, the charge was reduced to one of common assault because there was no evidence that Barratt had actually tried to fire the revolver. He was sentenced to three months imprisonment and bound over to keep the peace for two years.

CHAPTER 20

Deficiencies at the Office
1894

lbert Goodall's last words to his wife were 'May the Lord help you and have mercy on me'. They were in a letter that he posted to Fanny at their Albion Street address on 16 January 1894 before he drowned himself in the River Calder.

Albion Street, where Albert and Fanny Goodall lived, photographed in 2003.
The author

Goodall, who was forty-one, had worked for twenty-eight years as a clerk for the legal practice of Mander and Co in Thornes Lane. For many years his employer had been George Mander but he had continued with the firm after Mander's death under J R W Eldridge. At the time of his death he was employed as the cashier and, on his employer's behalf as the assistant clerk for the Wakefield Chamber of Commerce for which Eldridge was the secretary. He had a reputation for integrity and was always 'courteous and obliging'.

But Goodall's health had deteriorated in recent years. He had had rheumatic fever, two bad bouts of influenza, and then bronchitis. He complained of being 'devoid of energy'. In June 1893 he had a fall in the bedroom and cut his head so badly that he had to take two days off work.

On the Thursday evening before he took his life, Goodall told his wife that there was a 'deficiency' in 'the accounts'. He never went to the office the next day but arrived for work as usual on the Saturday and, amongst other tasks, engrossed a deed. His fellow clerk, William Scholey, asked him if he was all right and whether anything was the matter. Goodall's reply was simply that he did not know how he felt. He said nothing about any problem. However, he was expected to have a balance sheet

Reynolds, Stott and Haslegrave's mill. Albert Goodall's body was found close to the water wheel here. The John Goodchild Collection.

KINGS MILL

ready for the Chamber of Commerce the following week and it seems to have been this that was preying on his mind.

Fanny Goodall told the inquest that Sunday 14 January had been very happy. Albert, who sang in the choir at St Michael's Church, was so cheerful that she would never have dreamed of anything so terrible as his committing suicide.

It seems clear, though, that by lunchtime on Tuesday, Albert had made up his mind. He came home for the meal, as usual, but afterwards lingered over kissing his two younger children before saying, 'Good afternoon, love,' to Fanny. He stayed at the office until six in the evening. And that was the last time he was seen alive.

Fanny must have spent a wretched night after Albert failed to return home. By the morning post, the letter came from Albert:

Dear Fan, I fear my heart is breaking with this constant worry. There are deficiencies at the office and I cannot face them. There are a few pounds in the cash box and £6 5s Collins' rent. This rent is due to Mrs Mander. There are cheques in the cash box. I wanted a settling up with Mr Eldridge but I cannot enter into it. There is a cheque for £175 12s 4d in the cash box. My watch and chain are locked up in my drawer at the office. The office keys are also in this drawer. Oh, forgive me, love, for leaving you and the children in this manner. I feel distracted. Kiss them for me, and may the Lord help you and have mercy upon me. Your loving and distracted husband, Albert Goodall, Thornes Lane.

Albert's eighteen-year old son went straight to William Scholey with the letter. But Albert was not to be found at the office or anywhere else.

It was not until 8 February that his body was seen in the Calder close to the waterwheel at Reynolds, Stott and Haslegrave's flour mill in Thornes Lane. Constable Pratt, who took him from the water to the mortuary at the city police office, found 3s 1d (15p) in a pocket, together with a pair of gloves and a tuning fork.

The inquest was held later the same day. Had Albert taken money from work? Fanny said that if he had only carried on, the money would have been found somehow.

The concern of the jury was whether his family would receive a payment from the insurance company. Albert's life was insured for £25 with the Mutual Provident Alliance Society but death by self-murder meant exclusion from benefit. The coroner, Thomas Taylor, explained that it might be different if Albert killed himself whilst insane. Despite there being little evidence given of the state of his mind, the jury brought in that verdict.

CHAPTER 21

They Were Given Strychnine at Bath Time
1901

*F*oul Deeds and Suspicious deaths in Wakefield (2001) includes an account of how a shop assistant's mistake led to the agonised death of seventy-five-year old Mahala Learoyd at Lee Moor in 1866.

This was not the only time when an error in dispensing resulted in unnatural death locally. In 1901 three little girls in Normanton died after horrific convulsions when they were given strychnine instead of the medicine prescribed.

They were the only children of Joe Artle, a colliery blacksmith of 9 Mopsey Square, and his wife Annie.

Toddler Beatrice Maud, who was just twenty-two months old, was suffering from worms and on 21 February Dr William Mackenzie prescribed santonine. His dispenser, James Bryan Kennedy, weighed out the white powder from a white bottle. It seemed to do the child good. Two days later Annie Artle went back for more. Neither she, nor apparently Kennedy, noticed that this time he took down a blue bottle. He made up three small packets of the white powder it contained.

Annie gave Beatrice Maud another dose of powder at bath time that evening. In moments the child went into convulsions and shortly afterwards, even before Dr Mackenzie could get there, she died. The doctor put the death down to worms and the following Tuesday the little girl was buried.

But now four-year old Mary and three-year old Alice Gertrude had worms too. Less than a week after their sister's death, Annie gave each of her remaining girls one of the powders at bath time. The effect was immediate and terrible. Both children died within an hour after dreadful convulsions.

This time the West Riding coroner, Pelham Maitland, was told. He ordered the exhumation of little Beatrice Maud. When the inquest opened, at the *Hark to Mopsey* public house in Normanton on 27 February, Dr James Miles Harmon said that his preliminary view was that all three girls had died from taking strychnine. He needed confirmation and asked that the contents of their stomachs be sent to the Wakefield City analyst, Dr Edward Chaplin.

All three children were buried on Sunday 3 March in the graveyard at Normanton Parish Church.

The inquest resumed at the *Station Hotel*, Normanton, on 6 March. Chaplin confirmed that he had found strychnine in the bodies of each of the girls. Annie Artle said that, although she had once suspected the dispenser, Kennedy, of being drunk, she thought he was sober when he gave her the powders. Kennedy himself admitted that he must have taken down the strychnine bottle instead of its neighbouring santonine one.

The jury criticised Kennedy, observing that there was no excuse for his fatal mistake. However they brought in a verdict of misadventure on all three children.

But matters did not end there. People started talking, of course. Kennedy had got off scot-free. Was that right? The Chief Constable, Superintendent Crow, took a little time to think matters over but eventually, and in spite of the findings of the inquest, he decided to prosecute Kennedy. He arrested him on 25 March on a charge of causing the deaths of three children.

The case brought crowds to the Court House in Wood Street, Wakefield, when it was heard on 1 April before four magistrates. Crow explained that, despite the inquest verdict, he had a duty to ask the magistrates to decide whether Kennedy should be sent for trial at the Assizes on a charge of manslaughter.

The two bottles were produced in court. They were different in shape, size and colour. How could Kennedy have made such a mistake? Clearly there had been negligence, but did it amount to criminal negligence?

Kennedy was represented by a barrister, A W Bairstow. He pointed out that the bottles might be different but the powders they contained were very similar. Kennedy had been Dr Mackenzie's dispenser for more than four years. The case was like one where an experienced and reliable railway signalman, one day, inexplicably, sent a train down the wrong track and caused a crash.

The magistrates accepted that the degree of negligence did not amount to anything 'culpable'. Kennedy was freed and the Artles returned to their empty house.

CHAPTER 22

He Had Indeed 'Done It'
1902

When Esther Jarvis found a neighbour, William Williamson, wandering in the street in Belle Vue, Wakefield, on Saturday morning, 22 March, 1902, she urged him to come into her cottage to sit down. He went with her but kept saying, 'I have done it'. She was soon to discover that indeed he had – he had murdered the woman with whom he lived.

Williamson, who was sixty-three, was a stone mason by trade. He had come to Wakefield only three years previously

The Graziers *public house, Doncaster Road where the inquest was held into the death of Emily Illingworth.* The author

and worked for a time on the extension to Wakefield Cathedral but had fallen ill in 1901. He lived at Anchor Cottage, 6 Denmark Street, Belle Vue, with a woman named Emily Illingworth, some twenty years his junior, and thought by some to be his niece. The third member of the household was Emily's son Guy, a lad of sixteen who was described as 'odd' and 'of weak intellect'.

In the past Emily had worked as an upholsterer at Hall and Armitage's, New Wells, Wakefield, but she had become pregnant and had gone away to London. The child's father was a Wakefield man and paid maintenance for his son. In London Emily had met Williamson. In due course the pair had returned to the north, with Guy, to live in Portland Crescent, Leeds. After they moved to Wakefield, Guy had worked briefly at Fuller's, in Quebec Street, where he dressed firelighters, and then at Kendall's as an errand boy, but he had had no work since Christmas 1901 and spent most of his time in bed. He had the upstairs room at the cottage whilst Williamson and Emily shared a bed in the downstairs room. Guy lived on a little bread and butter and tea which his mother brought upstairs to him.

There can be little doubt that, with both Williamson and Guy unable to work, the household was, by March 1902, a wretched one. Charles Frederick Sampson of Charles Street, who gave evidence at the inquest into Emily's death, said that his wife had heard Emily and Williamson quarreling. Sarah Long, who, with her miner husband Charles, lived next to Williamson, said that she had heard him threatening to turn Emily out. But the most telling evidence came from Esther Jarvis. She had tried to help the family when Williamson was ill before Christmas. She took them food and gave them money for the rent.

Perhaps it was desperation that drove Williamson to kill Emily. We cannot know. Late on the evening of Friday 21 March Sarah Long heard them quarreling again. Charles Sampson heard some thumping and then a sound as if someone was cutting wood with an axe.

Early on Saturday morning Williamson went to the home of Police Sergeant Willows. He was still in bed and Williamson just muttered something about wanting to see him about his rheumatism and said that he would come back later. He never did. Meanwhile Esther Jarvis met him. At first he demanded to know the way to the 'cut' (the canal) but Esther urged him not to think of drowning himself but to go home with her to 2 East View. But when he announced not only that he had 'done it' but that they would hang him, she became fearful. Keeping Williamson with her, she asked her daughter, Charlotte, to go round to Williamson's house to 'let Emily know where he was'. Charlotte was equally fearful and asked her friend, fourteen-year old dressmaker's assistant, Marion Fowler, to go with her. It was Marion who entered the cottage and found Emily lying face downwards in a pool of blood. The body was already cold. Esther Jarvis continued calmly to detain Williamson whilst sending Charlotte and Marion for the police. Williamson was arrested and taken to the police station in Wakefield. His only remark was, 'It's awful, isn't it?'

Dr Roulston went to the cottage with Sergeant Willows to examine the body. The doctor said that she had been concussed with a blow from a piece of wood and then a large knife had been driven into her side and with another knife her throat had been cut.

Willows found that there was no food in the house other than part of a loaf, a little butter and a little tea. The place was cold and there was no coal. He found Guy still upstairs in bed, apparently unaware of what had occurred.

Williamson was brought before the West Riding magistrates on Monday 24 March. When charged he said he 'knew nothing about it'. An inquest was held at *The Graziers* public house, Doncaster Road, later the same day. Williamson was brought to the inquest but sat staring blankly throughout the proceedings. Evidence of the identity of the body was given by Emily's sister, Annie Gifford, of Meanwood Road, Leeds, who had learned of Emily's murder only when the police called at her house that morning. She described her sister as 'reserved but cheerful' and added that she did not drink.

The coroner, Pelham Maitland, attempted to establish whether Williamson was habitually violent. Guy told him that he never beat him or kicked him but he became distressed when he was asked whether he was afraid to go downstairs. Williamson rarely came upstairs, he said, and if he did he just 'cooed and smiled' at him. However the foreman of the Jury remarked that the boy had been so much abused that an officer from the Society for the Protection of Children had followed the family from Leeds to Wakefield.

The inquest jury brought a verdict of wilful murder against Williamson and he was committed for trial at Leeds Assizes. The case came before the court on 1 May. Williamson was invited to take a seat in the dock and the judge immediately raised the question of whether he was fit to plead. Evidence that he was 'profoundly demented' was given by Dr Henry Clark, the doctor at Wakefield Prison, and Dr William Bevan Lewis of the Pauper Lunatic Asylum (Stanley Royd). The jury was directed to find Williamson insane and unfit to plead, and the judge gave the order for him to be detained at His Majesty's pleasure.

CHAPTER 23

The Stabbing of a Thornes Bookmaker
1903

T he evening of 25 March, 1903 seemed just like many another convivial occasion at the home of thirty-year old George Henry Hall. He, his niece Alice and his wife Florence – the last nursing her baby – chatted with their friends, sending occasionally for some more beer though never in any quantity. So it is hard to understand why it should have ended in tragedy and why one of the Halls' guests should have stabbed his host to death.

Hall – generally known as Harry – was a bookmaker in business on his own and living at 7 Commercial Street, just off

The corner of Commercial Street and Thornes Lane, pictured in 2003. It was here that Harry Hall collected bets. The author

The former Wakefield City Police Station, a part of the one-time Tammy Hall, where the inquest was held into the death of George Hall. The author

Thornes Lane. With him lived his sixteen-year old niece, Alice Hall, who sometimes helped him in his business, his wife of two or three years (in giving evidence at the inquest Mrs Hall seemed vague about the date of the marriage and was sharply criticised by the coroner for this), and a baby.

There were two visitors at the Halls on 25 March. Frederick Thornton, son of the landlady of the nearby *Commercial Inn*, seems to have been a frequent 'dropper in'. The other was Hall's long-standing friend and perhaps protégé, Frederick Cooling. Cooling, who was thirty-nine, lived with his sister at 21 Wellington Street, Thornes Lane. He was a tall, powerfully-built man. He was a maltster's labourer by trade but he seems often to have done simple jobs for Hall, too, such as chopping wood, cleaning windows, or looking after the pony and trap which Hall kept for pleasure rather than for business, The pair had known each other for ten or twelve years and were sometimes to be seen together in the *New Inn* or the *Khedive Hotel* in Wakefield. Cooling did not assist at all with the betting business. This was normally carried on in the street, often on the corner of Thornes Lane and Commercial Street. Men would bring their bets, written on slips of paper, with their money, to Hall. Occasionally, he sent Alice to take the slips for him.

Betting houses had been made illegal by the Victorians in 1853 but betting itself was not illegal although the participants were not protected by law. The position was effectively reversed by the *Betting, Gaming and Lotteries Act* of 1963.

Cooling had done a day's work and had his tea before calling on his friend on the fatal evening. He spent some time dandling the Halls' baby but most of the evening was given to chat. On four occasions Hall suggested that Cooling fetched beer for them, always paying for it himself. Hall mentioned to Cooling that he would like him to clean the pony's harness as he wanted to take his family out on the coming Sunday.

It got late. Thornton left, Alice and Mrs Hall accompanying him to the door and staying chatting for a few moments. On her return, Mrs Hall began rocking the baby. She hinted to Cooling that it was time for him to go. Alice started to make ready for bed. Hall asked her to unlace his boots before she went upstairs. And at that moment, Cooling, his eyes – or so it was said – rolling wildly and in a white passion, asked, 'Am I to do it now?' took out his penknife, and stabbed Hall in the neck. The blood came out with such force that a stream shot across the room.

It was all over quickly. Cooling rushed out followed by the two women screaming for help. Hall died within two or three minutes despite the efforts by a local butcher named Tattershall to staunch the blood.

Dr Thomas Smith was summoned from Alverthorpe Road but Hall was already dead when he arrived. Police Sergeant Leonard Griffiths went to Cooling's home where he found him in bed. He ordered him to dress and took him to the police station. As they went, Cooling said, 'I suppose you are not going to kill me today. I suppose I have a few days to live.'

An inquest was held at the City Police Station on the evening of 27 March. Cooling was present, but appeared to take little interest in the proceedings. The inquest jury returned a verdict of wilful murder against him.

The doorway of the City Police Station with a sculpture of a policeman's head above it. The author

When the case was heard by the City magistrates, Cooling offered a defence. He had been cleaning out his pipe with his penknife, he said. Hall had remarked that it seemed 'very sharp' and Cooling held it out towards him saying, 'Have I to try it?' Hall said, 'Yes'. It was then, Cooling claimed, that he said, 'Am I to do it now?' Hall bared his neck but, as Cooling advanced the blade towards his friend, Hall twisted round and thus made contact with the knife.

The magistrates were having none of it. Florence Hall and Alice had been entirely clear about what they had seen and heard. Cooling was committed for trial at Leeds Assizes on the charge of murder. The case came to court on 11 May. Cooling said that the death was one of the biggest accidents that could have occurred. He would rather have killed himself than injured any member of Hall's family. His defending counsel pointed out that there was no motive for a wilful killing. In summing up, the judge made much of the fact that the evening had been a perfectly pleasant and happy one. No evidence had been given by anyone to show why Cooling should have got into a white passion.

Cooling was found not guilty and discharged. Perhaps the conversation about the knife which, allegedly, took place between Cooling and Hall, happened whilst Alice and Florence were seeing Thornton to the door. But what it if never took place at all?

CHAPTER 24

The First-Class Death of a Second-Class Baby
1906

To take a scantily-clad seven day old baby the breadth of the country by rail in the middle of winter seems the height of folly. Small wonder that the nameless child died of exposure long before the journey's end. But no one really cared about the anonymous little thing. Greed for money, and perhaps fear of the stigma of illegitimacy were in 1907 of more importance than a child's life.

The baby had been born on 18 December, 1906 to a Bradford woman, Annie Scruton, who kept a tobacconist's shop at 34 Church Bank. For her confinement the mother went well away from her place of business, to a nursing home at 63 Aughton Road, Birkdale, Southport where she was attended by Nurse Louisa Elizabeth Heyworth. There she agreed to pay Mary Ellen Robson, of 16 Brett Street, Quay Road, Bridlington, £10 to adopt the child. Mrs Robson seems to have made a business of taking unwanted children: she lived with her mother, a Mrs Milner, and already had four children in whatever care she actually provided.

Robson collected the baby on Christmas Eve. At Normanton, where she had to change trains and had a long wait ahead of her, she realised that the child was far from well. The assistant station-master, Mr Birkett, asked a porter to take Robson and the baby to the surgery of Dr James Stewart. Robson told the doctor that the child belonged to a friend of hers, a single woman living in Southport and that she was taking it to Bridlington so that the mother could return to work. Stewart expressed the view that the baby was suffering from exposure and that by the time the Bridlington train came in, at 3.10 am, it would be dead. But he seems to have done nothing for the child until at 11.30 pm he thought to tell the local police about the case. He may well have been prompted to act then by the terrible weather. It was a stormy night and six or seven inches of snow had fallen during the evening.

Inspector Aykroyd sent a sergeant to the railway station and went there himself about 12.30 am. By then the baby was dead, lying on a bench in the first-class waiting room.

The inquest into the little mite's death was opened at the *Talbot Hotel*, Normanton, on 28 December. Dr Sandiford said that the baby had clearly died of exposure. Inspector Aykroyd said that in his view the baby had been most inadequately clothed. Mrs Robson said that she wanted a baby because her own child had now reached school age. She sought to lay the blame for the child's death on the staff of the nursing home. Dr Newsham had said the baby was fit to travel, the matron,

Normanton Station about 1908. Norman Ellis collection

Nurse Heyworth, was clearly intoxicated, and the baby's mother had begged her to take the child away. The coroner, Pelham Maitland, was unimpressed by her evidence. He told her bluntly that she was lying. He added that a life had simply been thrown away and that to subject the baby to such exposure was 'wicked and cruel'. He decided to adjourn the hearing until Nurse Heyworth could defend herself. Meanwhile checks were made with the Southport police who described the nurse as a very respectable person, and with the Bridlington police to learn more about Mrs Robson herself.

When the inquest resumed, Nurse Heyworth, now married and Mrs Cotton, defended herself firmly: she had not been intoxicated and she had had no hand in the arrangements for the baby's adoption. A letter to the coroner from Dr Newsham confirmed that he had seen no reason why the baby should not travel provided that it was well wrapped up. Annie Scruton, the baby's mother, acknowledged that she had arranged the adoption and admitted that she had not made any inquiries as to the suitability of Robson to care for babies. Maitland invited the jury to consider whether subjecting the child to such a journey and to the exposure from which it died amounted to criminality. A verdict of manslaughter must have been an option. The jury, however, decided that death had resulted from exposure due to negligence on the part chiefly of Robson but also by the nurse and the baby's mother. Maitland told Mrs Robson that she was a lucky woman and that the jury had been 'merciful'. He upbraided Nurse Heyworth too for allowing Mrs Robson, who he termed a 'strange person', to take the child away, and he declared that the doctor should have used more common sense. His final words were that he hoped the Society for the Prevention of Cruelty to Children (which had been founded in 1884 and is now the National Society for the Prevention of Cruelty to Children) would take up the case.

CHAPTER 25

Killed by a Blow from a Policeman's Staff 1908

When Police Constable Elliott looked through the cottage window and saw Tom Harrison flourishing a bottle at one of his children and with another of them also at his mercy, he had no option but to rush inside and try to stop the madman killing the youngsters. But Harrison died, in the West Riding Pauper Lunatic Asylum in Wakefield, three months later as a result of the injuries the policeman inflicted on his skull.

Harrison was both a powerful and a violent man. It was said that it had once taken fourteen men to restrain him when he had one of his mad turns. He had already been committed to the asylum twice before the incident in 1908.

A part of the West Riding Pauper Lunatic Asylum, where Tom Harrison died, photographed in 2003 when it was being converted into flats. The author

Harrison was a weaver, living in Luddendenfoot, and was thirty-five at the time of his death. It was on 17 January that Harrison went berserk at home for the last time. He broke everything he could, whether crockery or furniture. He threw whatever came to hand into the fire. Then he seized a lamp and threw it at Sarah, his wife. She rushed out of the house in fear of her life. Meanwhile Harrison's father had gone to look for a policeman. Meeting Constable Elliott he reported that 'Our Tom' had gone mad again and that he had probably already murdered his wife. Hurrying back to the house they met Sarah. Elliott tried to enter but Harrison struck at him with a poker. The officer retreated but Sarah screamed that two of the children were in the house. Looking through the window, Elliott saw that Harrison had one of the children by the throat and heard him shout, 'If your mother does not come in, I'll murder the pair of you.'

Elliott went back in. There was a desperate struggle. Sarah Harrison managed to get the children out but, turning back, she saw the police officer on the ground with her husband on top of him. Elliott seemed barely able to breathe. Neighbours went to his aid. The struggle lasted half an hour during which Harrison threw the other men about 'like shuttlecocks'. Elliott hit Harrison twice with his staff and eventually, when more help arrived, he was overcome and tied up with ropes. He was covered in blood but attention was then given to his head wounds. He was reported as becoming much calmer and saying, 'Well, Elliott, you have done your duty. Shake hands.'

Harrison was immediately committed to the asylum where the wounds were stitched and he was diagnosed as suffering from 'acute melancholia'. Four weeks after his admission, an abscess developed in the wound. Despite careful treatment, his condition worsened and he died on 16 April.

So was the constable responsible for his death? At the inquest at the asylum on 18 April, Dr James Parker, the assistant medical officer, gave very clear evidence. When he had a bout of madness, Harrison was both very powerful and very dangerous. Then it would not have taken a very violent blow to cause the wounds. Sarah Harrison told the coroner that she had been convinced that her husband meant to kill her and the children.

The inquest jury recognised the compelling reasons for what Elliott did. Their verdict was 'Death from injuries to the skull caused by PC Elliott whilst engaged in a violent struggle. We exonerate PC Elliott from all blame. What he did was justified as a matter of self defence.' The coroner said that they should add that the action was also justified 'as a means of preventing crime'.

CHAPTER 26

Death of a Work-Shy Young Man 1908

There was not enough evidence to show how Charles Dilley came to be struck by a train but the case was of sufficient concern for an Inspector of Factories to attend the inquest and for the West Riding Iron and Coal Company, owners of the premises where the death occurred, to be represented by a solicitor as well as by the colliery manager. Dilley's relatives also retained a solicitor. Clearly there were questions both of blame and of possible compensation in the air.

In the course of the inquest, on 6 and 9 April 1908, it became clear that Dilley, who was twenty-five and lived with his mother, regularly absented himself from work at the East Ardsley company. Thomas Couse, the manager, said that he had spoken to Dilley about this the previous week after he had been off work for eight days. This was the third time that he had had occasion to reprimand him. He had warned the young man that he was now on twelve hours' notice and that, if he missed work again, he must consider himself finished. Nonetheless he had been off on Thursday 2 April. The next time Dilley put in an appearance, Couse would have sent him away and told him not to return.

It seemed that Dilley intended to go to work the following evening but no doubt his mother was anxious to make sure that he did so. He had spent most of the afternoon at the *Railway Hotel*, East Ardsley where, according to the landlord, Charles Hampson, he had three pints of beer. He asked for a further gill (half a pint) before he left about 6 pm but Hampson, knowing he had missed work the night before, refused to serve it. In the evening, he went back with his mother to the *Hotel* in his working clothes. He ordered a pint of beer but she asked the landlord not to supply it. He was not

The West Riding Iron and Coal Company's works, East Ardsley. The John Goodchild Collection.

'the worse for beer', she said at the inquest, but she did not think he needed it. He went home with her and left shortly afterwards, saying that he was going to work. She noticed, however, that he did not take any food with him. Her solicitor, T H Asquith, evidently realising that this might show something of his intent, quickly asked her whether this was unusual. She agreed that men often went to work without food, sending home for it later during the course of their shift.

The coroner, Pelham Maitland, seemed anxious too to shed light on Dilley's state of mind. Did he have a sweetheart? he asked. Was he thinking of getting married? He was dissatisfied generally with the mother's answers and said, 'You go round and round. You do not tell a straight tale. You are distressed, no doubt, at the loss of your son, but surely you could speak the truth.'

Ladles at the West Riding Iron and Coal Company's premises. The John Goodchild
Collection.

After Dilley left home, he set out on a footpath across colliery land but not in the direction of his work. There he was found at 10.45 pm by hawker William Reddington, lying with his head near the railway line which ran to the spoil heap. He was terribly injured. Reddington fetched help and Dilley was taken home on a stretcher.

Alfred Pickersgill, an engine driver at the plant, told the inquest that he had driven the engine, hauling a ladle, to the tip at about 10.30 pm. He had not felt any shock and there were no marks of blood either on the engine or on the ladle. He always sounded the whistle as the engine approached the nearby curve in the line.

Dr J J Jackson said that all the injuries had been to Dilley's head. There were wounds on the back and sides of the skull which was fractured. The wounds were consistent with Dilley's having been knocked down by a locomotive. There was no sign, though, on the body, boots or clothing, that Dilley had been dragged by the train.

Dilley died at 3 am on Saturday 4 April just a few hours after being taken home.

So Dilley might have died by accident. But, if so, what was he doing on a path leading away from work? Or he might have killed himself, but no explanation was given beyond the trouble he was in for 'skipping' work. The underlying question of why he stayed off so often was never formally raised. Or had the driver of the train been negligent? Was there an issue for the Inspector of Factories to pursue?

The jury rendered a verdict of 'accidentally knocked down but with insufficient evidence to show the circumstances'. It added a rider that the footpath should be diverted or even stopped up.

Eventually, at about 7.30 pm, Joseph Jones got him into an empty coal house at the back of the Free Church but, at the inquest, he was adamant that he had not 'thrown him' in there.

It was not until 9.30 pm that news reached Whitehead's son, George Henry (Harry) Whitehead, that his father was lying unconscious behind the chapel. At the same time, and at last, someone thought of calling the police. When young Whitehead found his father, Constable Hellewell was already there with a man identified only as 'Waffler'. Harry Whitehead called a cab and got his father home. He and his wife put him to bed, thinking that he was simply drunk and would 'sleep it off'. It was not until the following morning that Harry sent for a doctor. Even then, Dr Macfarlane came to the same conclusion as Harry, that Whitehead would be all right once he had slept long enough. Dr Macfarlane came back on the morning of Monday 22 June and issued a prescription for medicine to be collected from the surgery. He returned the same evening but made no further suggestion as to the care of the unconscious man. On Tuesday 23 June Macfarlane brought a colleague, Dr Finch, for a consultation. The doctors then, at last, said that Whitehead should go to Clayton Hospital, in Wakefield. He was taken there that evening in the Snydale ambulance.

Harry Whitehead visited his father regularly but said that the elderly man was able to speak to him only once, on 15 July, when he said 'Good afternoon'.

Whitehead died on Monday 27 July. That evening George Knapper was arrested and charged with manslaughter. He was brought before the West Riding magistrates in Pontefract and was remanded in custody.

An inquest into Whitehead's death was opened at Clayton Hospital the following day. Knapper was present in police custody. The coroner, Pelham Maitland, was in a typically acerbic mood. It was, he said, disgraceful that Whitehead was left to lie for hours in the coal house. 'Where,' asked the foreman of the jury, were the police?' Maitland rounded on him. The police could not have known he was there, he said, and went on, 'The police are not witches. If you want them at every corner you will have quite some rates to pay!'

The Jubilee Hotel, *Featherstone, in 2003.* The author

When the inquest resumed two days later, one witness admitted that Whitehead had been hidden away because everyone thought he was drunk and they wanted to keep him out of the way of the police. As more witnesses gave their evidence, Maitland said that he had 'never heard such a mixed up tale' in his life.

The pathological evidence was given by Dr McRobb, house surgeon at Clayton Hospital. Whitehead had died, he said, from compression of the brain following an injury to the head. The coroner observed that there must be a strong presumption that it was the blow in the *Jubilee Hotel* that caused Whitehead's death but that Whitehead had also been roughly handled after this – he had been 'trailed about' to keep him out of the way of the police.

Although Maitland said that he need not do so, George Knapper chose to make a statement at the inquest himself. He said that he had gone to the bar to get two pints of beer, had caught Whitehead accidentally with his shoulder, and then saw him lying on the floor. He was 'never more surprised in his life' than when he was charged by the police.

The jury accepted that the immediate cause of death was compression of the brain and that this was caused by Whitehead's being pushed by George Knapper and falling against a seat. They added, however, that the death was a matter of misadventure as Knapper had only been trying to

The former chapel in Featherstone where Levi Whitehead was hidden from the police in a coal store. The author

keep Whitehead from troubling him. They added (importantly for the licensee) that the management of the hotel was free from any blame and that there was no reflection on the conduct of the police.

But of course Knapper was already facing a charge of manslaughter. The day after the inquest concluded, his father, Joe Knapper, applied for bail on his behalf. This was granted and he was bound over for £5.

Knapper came before the magistrates again on Saturday, 1 August. He was again remanded on bail with the explanation that the court needed advice from the county solicitor as Knapper had been charged with manslaughter but the inquest verdict had been one of misadventure.

A week later the legal advice was that the charge should be withdrawn. Knapper was free.

CHAPTER 28

It should have been her Wedding Day 1909

No doubt whoever assisted Florence Fordham to miscarry had meant to help her. But Florence died and at a resumed inquest at Clayton Hospital on 4 November 1909 the jury decided that 'deceased was wilfully murdered by person or persons unknown attempting by unlawful measures to procure an abortion and so setting up peritonitis from which she died.' She was just twenty-one.

Florence lived with her parents and their younger children at 21 Smyth Street. She had worked for four years at the Tadcaster Tower Brewery in Southgate where she had met and become engaged to Charles Bradley, of Globe Yard, the foreman of the bottling plant. For a time Bradley had moved in with the Fordhams. More recently Florence had worked at E P Shaw's aerated mineral water works. There she had become involved with a married man, Charlie Mitchell. At Whitsuntide 1909, Florence and Mitchell were thought to have gone away together, possibly to Bristol. They had returned after nine days. Bradley declared that he would still marry Florence if she could prove that she had not been with Mitchell.

In August, Florence confided in her aunt, Mrs Olive France, of 10 Grove Street, that she was pregnant and that the father of the child was Bradley. It seems that, without consulting Bradley, Florence arranged for them to be married in Wakefield Cathedral on 28 October. The banns were read. Bradley made no objection and in fact agreed to rent a house for them in Talbot and Falcon Yard. Later he claimed that he had not known Florence was pregnant until his sister told him of the gossip she had picked up.

On the Monday before Florence died, she received a letter from Bradley. He wrote to say that he could not 'go through' with the marriage. The girl went white. Then she went, as she

Wakefield Cathedral where Florence was to have been married. The author

had been doing each day, to her aunt's. No one was prepared to admit at the inquest exactly what happened then or in the next couple of days. Florence wrote to Bradley asking him to meet her at the bottom of Smyth Street but he did not come. On Thursday Florence fainted whilst peeling some potatoes. The following day, Friday 22 October, she was worse and her mother sent for Dr Thomson. He was clear that she had had a miscarriage and he asked whether she had been 'interfered with'. She insisted that she had not. Thomson advised that she should be sent to Clayton Hospital but she was reluctant to go and her mother refused to let her be taken there; she had already had one child die in the hospital, she said.

That evening, however, Florence's condition deteriorated and Dr Clayton was called in. She was taken to hospital at 10.15 pm. She was conscious when she was admitted and told Dr Lister, the house surgeon, that Bradley was 'responsible for all this'. The doctor asked whether Bradley had sought to procure an abortion but she said he had not and denied that any instrument had been used on her. She died the following day without revealing anything more.

An inquest was opened on 25 October and adjourned until 28 October, which was to have been Florence's wedding day.

The jury was told that a post-mortem examination showed that an instrument certainly had been used and that the girl's womb had been perforated. It would have taken a degree of violence. Dr Thomson suggested that something like a crochet needle could have done the damage. The immediate cause of death was peritonitis.

The coroner criticised the other witnesses for holding evidence back. He warned both Mrs France and Mrs Fordham that a murder had been committed and that they must tell the inquest all they knew. He was himself sure that they were lying when they claimed to be ignorant of the details of how the girl came to miscarry. Florence's killer, or killers – for that is what they were, although their intentions were no doubt good – remained unidentified.

CHAPTER 29

But How Did the Baby Die?
1910

I t is hardly surprising that Annie Varley tried to explain her bulky abdomen by claiming that she had a 'floating tumour' She was unmarried and already had two young children. There had been a third but this had died in infancy. She and her father were penniless and homeless and no one was likely to take them in with another baby on the way.

But Annie gave birth to the 'floating tumour' one Saturday in February 1910.

Annie was twenty-seven. Her mother had died nine years previously and from that time Annie had kept house for her father, William, or at least shared his lodgings. William, who, in 1910 was sixty-seven, had been employed at Dewsbury Post Office for many years but had then gone on to work for a milk purveyor in Wakefield. Latterly he had lived precariously by selling his 'poetic effusions'.

In January 1910 William, Annie, and the two children, Alice and Harry, were living in Ossett. They left their lodgings there and sought refuge with one of Annie's brothers, George Edward Varley, who was a railway porter at Mexborough but who lived in Walton. George's household was already crowded and his wife was ill. There was a quarrel and the newcomers were turned out. It was late January and a cold and snowy night. Annie knocked at the door of David and Mary Swaine in Soaphouse Yard, Walton, and asked them to let the children get warm. Although the Swaines had only a two-roomed cottage and they had two children of their own, they took the refugees in, initially offering to let them stay for the weekend. David Swaine explained later that they just could not let the little children suffer.

The four Varleys stayed on. Annie and her children shared one bed in the upstairs room; the Swaines and their children,

The Barnsley Canal at Walton where the baby's body was found. The John Goodchild Collection.

aged five and sixteen months, shared the other bed. William Varley slept on a couch downstairs. Rumours circulated in Walton that Annie was pregnant.

On Saturday 19 February Annie said that she felt unwell. She stayed in bed. William went out. In the evening Mr and Mrs Swaine put their children to bed and went into Wakefield to the market getting home about 10 pm. When David Swaine went to bed he noticed a blood clot on the bedroom wall. He pointed it out to his wife but she made no comment. Annie stayed in bed most of the next day although, it seems, she ate three good meals including a dinner of rabbit pie with three pieces of Yorkshire pudding. She got up in the evening looking very noticeably slimmer. 'Your stoutness has soon disappeared,' David remarked, adding, 'It goes to show you are not as people said'.

Two days later, Robert Wood, keeper at Walton Low Lock, saw a baby's legs sticking up out of the canal. Constable Steele was summoned from Crofton. The baby had been wrapped in a curtain and then in brown paper. The bundle had been tied up with string and then a rope, with a 14lb stone at one end of it, had been tied to the string. There was a bootlace round the baby's neck. The policeman took the body to the *New Inn* and the coroner was informed. David Swaine, who was working on the new school in Walton, heard the news the following day. He told Annie about it. All she said was that it might have belonged to one of the boat people. However, David told Constable Steele of his suspicions. Dr J M Herman was brought from Wakefield to examine Annie Varley. He was sure that she had given birth in the last few days. In fact her breasts were swollen with milk. She was arrested 'on suspicion'. She admitted that she had been delivered the previous Saturday. She said that the baby had lived only for a few moments. She had wrapped it up, put it in a bag and asked a man who was passing by to drop the bag into the canal.

Annie was taken back to Walton the next day, Wednesday 23 February, to attend the inquest. This opened at the *New Inn*. Dr Herman gave evidence that the baby had lived, if only for a short time, and had died from suffocation, probably by being strangled rather than drowned. The inquest was adjourned but

The New Inn, *Walton, where an inquest was held into the death of Annie Varley's baby.* The author

that afternoon Annie was charged at Wakefield with wilful murder. She pleaded guilty and was remanded to Armley gaol.

David and Mary Swaine looked about their house. Mary found bloodstained sheets and clothing at the bottom of her 'peggy tub'. Under Annie's bed they found a carpet bag which had blood stains on it and which contained more bloodstained clothing.

A local coal miner, John Goose, recalled seeing William Varley walking by the canal with just such a carpet bag.

On Friday 25 February, William too was arrested. He was charged with being an accessory to murder.

The inquest should have resumed the following Tuesday but the prison doctor said that Annie was unfit to attend.

When finally the inquest was held, the coroner, Pelham Maitland, speculated that both William and Annie might be implicated in the murder. Perhaps she had strangled the child and her father had finished it off by drowning it. So prompted, the jury brought a verdict of wilful murder against both William and Annie.

The pair came before West Riding magistrates Percy Tew and J W Walker on 9 March. Dr Herman again said that death could have been caused either by strangulation or drowning and that he did not think that the child could have bled to death. Varley admitted that he had tied the bootlace round its neck. The Varleys' solicitor insisted that there was no clear evidence as to how the baby had died and that the only safe charge was one of failing to register a birth. However the magistrates committed both father and daughter for trial on the capital charge at Leeds Assizes.

There is no report of their being tried, however. It is always possible that the Grand Jury decided that there was sufficient uncertainty about the baby's death for the case to be dropped.

CHAPTER 30

Death After a Game of Dominoes
1910

When John William Mansford was carried home insensible on an August Saturday night, his brother and sister-in-law left him lying outside until morning. It had happened often before when he had been drunk. But this time he had a fractured skull and the following day he died.

Mansford, who was thirty four, was in 1910 a miner, working at Park Hill Colliery. He had served as a young man in the 2nd battalion of the Yorkshire and Lancashire regiment but for the past nine years he had lodged with his brother and his family in one of the yards off South Street, near Kirkgate Station, Wakefield. He was described as healthy and strong but quick tempered; it took only a little beer to make him quarrelsome.

On the evening of 20 August, Mansford went to the *New Dusty Miller* public house in Charles Street, not far from his home. At some time in the evening Mansford's brother, James, joined him there. Shortly after ten o'clock, George Carver, a thirty-seven year old fitter who lived at a lodging house in Park Street, came into the pub and began a game of dominoes with John Willows. Mansford offered to bet Carver the sum of 2d that Willows would beat him and laid the money on the table. Carver accepted the bet but, as he had no coppers on him, he put a sixpenny piece down. Willows won the game and Mansford pocketed the full eightpence. Carver demanded fourpence back. Mansford responded, 'You may wait till you get it'. However his brother, fearing a quarrel, advised him to hand the money over to avoid trouble. The landlord, George Norman, sensing a problem, ordered the two men out. Shortly afterwards he called, 'Time'.

There were conflicting accounts of what happened next but even Carver himself agreed that he struck Mansford a blow which felled him and that Mansford hit his head hard on the flagstones and lay on his back unconscious, and like a log. Someone brought a bowl of water and another drinker, Herbert Booth, who was a labourer at Brotherton's chemical works, tried to get Mansford to drink, but he remained insensible. Booth and three others, George Hodgson, Thomas Robertshaw and William White, lifted him up and carried him home. There was no one in so, as he was now coming round, they sat him on the steps leading up to the house door. He told them he would be alright, adding, 'God bless you.'

Very possibly, when they came home, James Mansford and his wife, Betsy, saw him there although they both said in sworn evidence that they had not done so. They both entered the house by the door into the cellar kitchen but must have passed the front steps to get there. James said that when he went in his brother was nowhere to be seen. He assumed he had gone up to his bedroom. Betsy said that she had been to the market with her son and on the way home, about 11o'clock, had seen a crowd outside the public house. Mrs Robertshaw told her that her husband had been carried home nearly dead. She had run to the house and seen that John William, and not James, was propped up on the front steps. She went back to Charles Street, found James, and urged him to come home. He said that he had been 'having some bother' with a young man and told her to go back home. He joined her soon afterwards. John William was no longer to be seen.

The next morning, James woke to the sound of loud snoring. He looked through the bedroom window and called to his wife, 'Our Dobbler's laid flat in the floor'. It was only then that he told Betsy that John William had been knocked out by George Carver. Mansford was again unconscious and was bleeding from an ear and from the nose. The couple got him into the cellar kitchen and – but not until 9.15 am – James went for the police. Dr W K Clayton was summoned and diagnosed a fractured skull. Mansford was taken to Clayton Hospital by police horse ambulance but he died at 4.45 pm without gaining consciousness.

Carver was arrested before Mansford's death and charged initially with causing grievous bodily harm. He was present at the inquest at the City Police Station on the evening of 22 August, in the care of Inspector Tattersfield, where he was reported as being a 'respectably dressed, pale-faced, dark complexioned, small man'. The inquest jury found that Mansford had been killed by George Carver. He was remanded in custody until 2 September when, at the City Court, he was committed for trial at the Assizes but allowed bail on his own £40 and £20 from each of his two brothers.

At Leeds Assizes on 29 November he was found not guilty.

CHAPTER 31

Everyone Concerned Broke the Law
1910

In the view of Coroner Pelham Maitland, everyone concerned with the deaths and burial of Ernest Asquith's new-born twins was either stupid or wicked or both.

Asquith was a miner and he and his wife lived at 2 Calder Terrace, Bottomboat. Mrs Asquith had expected to be confined close to Christmas 1910 and had made arrangements with a qualified midwife, Sarah Anne Spurr, to attend her then. But on the evening of Friday 23 September, three months prematurely, she went into labour. Asquith fetched her sister, Norah How, at four in the morning and went for the midwife at half-past five. The baby boys were born shortly afterwards, within ten minutes of each other. Neither lived for more than another ten or fifteen minutes.

Mrs Spurr seems to have taken charge. She told Asquith to get a coffin but said nothing whatever about the need to register the births or to obtain a death certificate. Asquith went to see Harry Bell, a joiner and undertaker, at his premises in Ferry Lane, Stanley. Bell told him that there need be only one 'box' for the babies but, as they had lived for a little time, they should have a 'proper' funeral.

Asquith then went off to a miners' rally.

Bell's assistant, Joseph Ward, made the little coffin and took it to Calder Terrace where, when Mrs Spurr had laid the babies in it, he screwed down the lid. He then took the coffin to William Shepherd, the sexton at Stanley Church, and asked him to bury the twins. Shepherd was reluctant to do so without appropriate papers but, after Ward had left, he decided that, as Bell was a respectable undertaker, it would be all right and the papers would no doubt follow, so he carried out the interment. There was an area of the graveyard set aside

The Thatched House, *Stanley, where an inquest was held into the deaths of the Asquith twins.* The author

for still-born babies. But, of course, the Asquith twins were not still-born.

Meanwhile it chanced that Dr George Wiggin, of Methley, called at Mrs Spurr's. She told him about the premature twins and asked him to write a death certificate. Not having seen the babies for himself, he was very reluctant to do so, but Mrs Spurr assured him that they had been premature and he wrote out a paper which both he and the midwife signed. She took the certificate to Shepherd.

Now, realising that the babies had lived and very worried about the interment, Shepherd went to see his vicar, Reverend J B Bolland. Bolland contacted both the Registrar, Mr Druce, and the police. On Monday 26 September the little coffin was disinterred and Dr W B Evans of Stanley conducted a post-mortem examination. An inquest was held at the *Thatched House*, Stanley, on Tuesday 27 September. It was attended by the West Riding Medical Officer, Dr J R Kaye, Dr Wiggin, Mr Druce the Registrar, Inspector Wrangham, Sergeant Taylor of the West Riding Police, and the Reverend J B Phillips on behalf of the vicar, as well as by the midwife, Sarah Spurr, joiner Harry Bell, his assistant Joseph Ward, the sexton, William Shepherd, and the babies' father.

Pelham Maitland explained the reasons, as he saw them, for holding an inquest. There had been indecent haste in getting the babies buried, the interment had taken place without either a death certificate or burial order, there must be grave suspicions as to the causes of the twins' deaths, he feared there might have been foul play, and in sum the whole affair was 'shrouded in mystery'. 'If people will do stupid things,' he said, 'it is their own fault if they have to take the consequences.'

The twins' father, Ernest Asquith, explained that the babies were very premature but that, since they had lived for ten or fifteen minutes, the undertaker thought they should have a proper burial. He had called his sister to look after his wife and, setting off to the rally, he had left word that if the undertaker came, he could screw up the coffin. He had known

Stanley Church. The twins were buried in the graveyard and then exhumed. Wakefield Historical Publications.

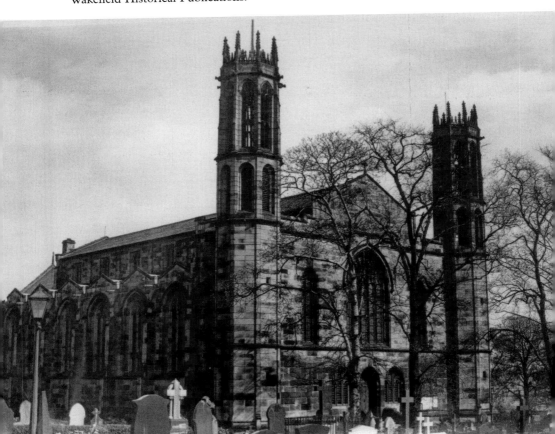

no more of the matter until a detective called on him on the Monday.

Mrs Spurr admitted that she had lacked the presence of mind to tell the father that the deaths would need to be registered. This earned the rebuke from Maitland that she had made a 'horrible mess'.

It was Bell's turn for a reprimand next. He claimed that he had told Asquith that the babies would need a proper funeral but that Asquith had insisted that Mrs Spurr thought this was not necessary as they were only six-month children. Maitland remarked, 'If this is the way you do your business, you had better shut up'.

William Shepherd, who had worked as the sexton for over thirty years, was next in line for the coroner's condemnation. When he had given his evidence, Maitland observed, 'This was very wicked. These children were not still-born. You deprived them of a proper funeral service. Disgraceful.'

Only Dr Evans escaped censure! His evidence was quite clear. The babies had died because they were premature. They could not have lived for more than a few minutes and their lungs had not inflated properly.

The jury returned a verdict accordingly.

CHAPTER 32

The Dire Consequences of a Separation Order 1910

mma Linford was taking a terrible risk when she obtained a separation order from her husband, George, at Wakefield city court on 17 October, 1910. She and George, a plasterer by trade, lived at Mollacrees Yard, Kirkgate. They had been married in 1874 at Holy Trinity Church and had six adult children. But for some years prior to the separation, George had not worked and the couple depended on their children for maintaining the home. Moreover George had grown increasingly violent and Emma claimed to be afraid of him.

Carlton Street, Wakefield, where George Linford shot his wife. The author

Emma moved to Carlton Street. But on the morning of 22 October, George sought her out and shot at her, injuring her lip and hand. He then fled but was arrested in Huddersfield. He was tried at Leeds Assizes on 23 November and sentenced to three years' penal servitude.

CHAPTER 33

An Open Verdict
1915

Coroner Pelham Maitland was given to bullying the witnesses who appeared at his inquests, and frequently accused them of lying. There was no question of his showing gentleness to a woman who had just lost her child, especially if he suspected that she might have been responsible for its death. He went as far as he could, on the basis of the evidence, to condemn Esther Ann Shortland, of 25 Town End, Ossett, whose two month old baby, Jane, died on Saturday 13 March 1915.

Esther was married to Ernest Shortland, formerly an assistant water inspector for Ossett Corporation, but then a private in the second battalion of the King's Own Yorkshire Light Infantry. She had had ten children, seven of them still living. She told the inquest that she had an income of £1 6s (£1.30) a week from the army and a further 15s (75p) a week from the Corporation. She had gone to bed at 9.30 pm on Friday 12 March, she said stressing that she was sober. At two in the morning she had woken and put the baby to her breast. Then she had slept again with the baby in the crook of one arm and her nineteen-month old toddler in the crook of the other. When she woke again at 4.30 am the baby was dead.

Dr J D Gray had made a post-mortem examination the same day. The baby was well nourished, he said, but had died of suffocation.

Maitland insisted that Esther was lying and that her beer jug had been filled twice on the Friday evening. Esther said it could not have been hers but Maitland told her to be quiet and remarked that in that case it was someone else's full jug that had been sent to her house. Constable Smith reported an interview he had had with the landlord of the *Coopers' Arms* who had admitted that, although Esther had not herself been

The Cooper's Arms, *Ossett, where Esther Shortland's beer jug was regularly filled.*
The author

to the public house, her beer jug had been sent two or three times on the Friday evening with one of her sons. He could recognise the individual jugs of all his customers, he said.

There was clearly no evidence to indicate that Esther had wilfully killed her baby. However, Maitland embarked on a lengthy address to the jury in which he made much of the fact that Esther was receiving forty-one shillings a week to keep her children and was spending it on drink. She should have been prosecuted, he said, and the money taken from her. She was undoubtedly 'in beer' on the fateful night, he insisted. Was this really accidental suffocation or did the baby die because its mother was the worse for drink, he asked. He then suggested, and obtained, an open verdict.

CHAPTER 34

Did the 'Illegal Instrument' Cause her Death?
1915

Before it became legal to terminate a pregnancy, at least in some circumstances, in 1967, many an inquest was held into the death of a woman for whom a 'back street' abortion had proved fatal. The coroner would inquire closely into whom the dead woman had visited and who had 'procured' the miscarriage but witnesses would plead ignorance. So there would frequently be a verdict of wilful murder against a person or persons unknown.

The case of Fanny Hill, however, was different. Fanny, who was thirty-five, was the wife of Abraham Hill, a Streethouse boot repairer. When in the summer of 1915 she found herself in 'a certain condition', her sister in law, Edith Hill, took her to see a neighbour, Sarah Ann Alton, of 2 Budholm Cottages, Streethouse, who was thought to have useful contacts. In fact Sarah had given lodging the previous year to one Sarah Wilshaw who had become pregnant by a young German man who had then been interned at the outbreak of war. Sarah Wilshaw had visited Jane Seggar, 3 Hainsworth Street, Tong Lane, Leeds, and had duly lost the unwanted baby.

Sarah Alton organised things for Fanny. She wrote to Mrs Seggar who, she said, claimed to be a doctor, and she also contacted Caroline Carrington, the wife of a Methley miner, who had a reputation as a herbalist. Caroline gave Fanny some pills. Jane Seggar used what was always termed 'an illegal instrument'.

Back home in Streethouse, Fanny became gravely ill. On 19 September, the Featherstone based Dr Elder was called in and directed that she be taken to Clayton Hospital where

Dr J Walker operated on her. But on 22 September Fanny died from blood poisoning.

Meanwhile Seggar had been arrested by Leeds City Police on a charge of performing an illegal operation and remanded to Armley Gaol.

Coroner Pelham Maitland opened an inquest into Fanny's death but adjourned it in order to obtain permission from the Home Office for Seggar to be present. It was resumed on 6 October with Seggar in the charge of two prison officers. Inspector Bradley of Leeds City Police told the inquest how he had called on Seggar and she had admitted to the initial charge and had produced the 'illegal instrument' she had used. The jury brought a verdict of wilful murder against Seggar and she was committed for trial at Leeds Assizes.

The critical question for the Assize jury was whether it was the use of this instrument that had brought about the blood poisoning which caused Fanny's death. Dr Bullock admitted that he could not say whether septicaemia had already been present before Fanny visited Seggar. Inevitably after that, Seggar was found not guilty of the charge of murder.

CHAPTER 35

Her Mother had Suspicions
1918

T he small community of Bottomboat must have been traumatised in the summer of 1918 when there were two, wholly unconnected, murders.

The earlier took place on 29 June when sixteen-year old Mary Cooke took the life of her new-born baby at her home in Co-operative Row. Mary's mother said at the inquest on 23 July that she had 'had her suspicions' about her daughter's condition and had frequently criticised her for staying out late, but the girl had always denied that she was pregnant and had accused her of 'always thinking the worst'.

Mrs Cooke was out shopping on the morning of 29 June when Mary gave birth. Her eight-year old brother, Philip, was at home when Mary called from her bedroom and asked him to bring her a knife. Philip said at the inquest that there was something 'squeaking' in the room when he went up. His sister later came downstairs, he said, and went into the front room. She then returned to bed and, soon afterwards, horrified Philip by calling to him 'Go to the butcher's for my mother. I am dying.'

Back at home, Mrs Cooke sent for Dr J T Cameron, of Lake Lock, to attend her daughter. She herself looked in the cupboard in the front room where she found the dead baby wrapped in newspaper. There were deep cuts in its cheeks and its throat had been slit from side to side. The bloodstained knife lay on the floor. Dr Cameron called Constable Winfield. The police surgeon, Dr J W Taylor, conducted the post-mortem examination and confirmed that the baby had had an 'independent existence' and had died from wounds to its throat.

Ten days later Mary was formally charged at the police office in Methley with having killed the baby.

Bottomboat in 2003. The author

The inquest jury returned a verdict of wilful murder. Mary was then brought before the county magistrates court on 25 July and committed for trial at Leeds Assizes.

Newspapers give only a brief report of the proceedings at the Assizes. The trial took place on 27 November. Without the benefit of reading the evidence it seems strange that Mary was found not guilty and was discharged. It was reported that she was to be looked after by the wife of a miner at Conisbrough. This is another tantalising fact.

CHAPTER 36

Yet More Dead Babies
1918

In the past, inquests into the deaths of new-born babies were frequent. In 1918, for example, Coroner Pelham Maitland held at least three such inquests. On 26 March there was an inquest at Wakefield City Police Station into the death of a male child born to twenty-year old Doris Heslop, a munitions worker who lodged with Mary Ann Asquith at Grove Street. Evidence was given by Mrs Asquith and by Mary Eccles who claimed to be a friend of the mother. Doris had previously been in lodgings at 77 Northgate but had moved to Grove Street in January 1918. She went out to work regularly until Wednesday 20 March but had then claimed that she was ill and had stayed in her room. Mrs Asquith tried to persuade her to see a doctor but Doris refused. She remained in bed through the weekend. Then on Monday 25 March, Mary Eccles, who had heard that Doris was 'in trouble', had called asking to see her. Mrs Asquith said, 'There's something mysterious about her,' and the two had gone to her room together. Mary stayed with her friend and drew the truth out of her. Her dead baby lay in a bundle in the corner of the room. Doris was taken to the workhouse infirmary. The medical evidence at the inquest was that the baby had lived for a short while but that it had died from lack of attention either at the time of birth or afterwards. Maitland adjourned the inquest until Doris could be present.

A further inquest took place at the Police Station on 26 June into the death of the child born to sixteen year old Georgina Farrington the previous Saturday. Georgina lived at 3 Fleece Yard, Brook Street, and worked as a rover at Haley's mill in Alverthorpe Road. Her sister, Sarah, worked there too. Both girls were at work on the morning of Saturday, 20 June, when Georgina claimed to be ill. She was sent home, Sarah going with her. The pair reached the bottom of Westgate when Georgina could walk no further. She collapsed on an ash-heap. Sarah ran back to Westgate End House to call for Dr Reader but he was out and Sarah ran back again to Georgina. By that time Georgina's baby had been born. Mother and baby were taken in by a Mrs Wilson who lived nearby and

Westgate End House from which Dr Reader was summoned to attend to Georgina Farrington. Author's collection

who, it was reported, treated the girl with great kindness. Sarah now found Dr Reader at home and he came to attend to the mother and child. He advised Sarah to get them home quickly and a taxi was called. Despite such care, the baby died at eight o'clock that evening. At the inquest Sarah said that no one had known of her sister's pregnancy. Coroner Maitland gave his view that Georgina was 'very much to blame'. She should, he said, have confided in someone. The medical evidence was that the child would have lived if proper arrangements had been made for the confinement. The verdict was that the baby died 'from congestion of the lungs through a chill contracted at birth on an ash-heap at Westgate End.'

On 2 July the inquest was at Wakefield City Police Station. The dead baby was the daughter of Pamela Percival of 10 Volunteer Yard, Kirkgate. Mrs Percival was married but her husband was serving with the armed forces in Palestine and had not been home for two and a half years. Pamela gave birth alone on Saturday night, 29 June. She and the baby were later looked after by a neighbour, Mrs Pomfret, and by Probationer Nurse Abbott from the Wakefield workhouse infirmary. But the baby died the following afternoon. Dr Mary Purdie conducted the post-mortem and concluded that the child had died from partially collapsed lungs and from want of attention at birth. The jury accepted that as their verdict. I have found no record of any blame being attached to the mother.

CHAPTER 37

He Was Willing to Swing
1918

John William Walsh never denied that he had killed his paramour, Ruth Elizabeth Moore. In fact a few hours after he had strangled her, on 11 July 1918, he went to her neighbour's house to announce that he had 'done her in'.

Ruth Moore, who was forty-two when she died, was married to a Suffolk pig and poultry dealer but had left him eight years previously. She had kept house in Occold, in Suffolk, for one Arthur Everson and had 'kept company' with his cousin, William Mills. Everson's sister, Elizabeth Seymour, had moved to Wakefield in 1913 and Ruth and William had followed. They came to live in Major Street at Thornes. William found work as a maltster's labourer at Sutcliffe's.

But then came the Great War. William was called up as a reservist and was taken prisoner during the retreat from Mons. Although still formally married to Moore and, indeed, receiving financial support from him, Ruth got an allowance from Sutcliffe's.

Ruth moved to Outwood and found other company in the person of John William Walsh. At the inquest into her death, Mrs Mary Day, who lived at Smith Street, Church Lane, Outwood, said that Ruth and Walsh had lived close by and that she regularly heard them quarrelling. In October 1916 Ruth ran out of the house screaming and claiming that Walsh was trying to murder her. Shortly afterwards, in December 1916, Ruth moved, with Walsh, then aged thirty-four, and his brother Martin as her lodgers, to Calder Terrace, Bottomboat. Neighbours again heard frequent quarrels. Martin Walsh left in January 1918 and in May, after yet another quarrel, Ruth told Walsh himself to leave. He returned four weeks later and threatened Ruth with a razor. However he went away again and was not seen in the vicinity for another couple of weeks.

Then, on 10 July, Ernest Berry, a milkman living at Tate's Buildings, saw Walsh again hanging about in the Bottomboat area. Neighbours warned Ruth that he was in the vicinity but she said that she was not afraid. She locked the house as usual that evening and went to bed.

The same night, Walsh got in through a cellar grate. At about five in the morning he strangled Ruth as she lay asleep. He made a somewhat feeble attempt to cut his own throat. Four hours later he went to the next door house where he asked Jane Ann Lockwood for a cigarette and told her what he had done.

Mrs Lockwood seems to have remained remarkably calm. She advised Walsh to give himself up to the police and he did just that. He called on Constable Winfield and was arrested.

Walsh was brought before the county magistrates on 24 July. One of Ruth's neighbours, Sarah Bostock, said that, although there were dreadful quarrels, Walsh seemed very fond of Ruth. But the prosecuting solicitor pointed out the evidence of previous attacks on Ruth's life and urged that the crime had been premeditated.

Terrace houses at Bottomboat in 2003. The author

Walsh was tried at Leeds Assizes on Saturday 30 November on two charges – that of murder and of attempted suicide. He was found guilty and sentenced to death. Asked if he had anything to say, he replied, 'I can only say I am guilty but it is through sickness. I am upset. I am willing to swing. That is all I have to say.'

Walsh was executed at Armley gaol on 17 December 1918.

CHAPTER 38

Death at a Dance
1920

Nineteen-year old Jane Darwell must have felt very excited as she hurried home from her work at *The Royal Oak* in Crofton on the evening of 25 October, 1920 to get changed to go to the Crofton Cricket Club dance. She could not know that it would be her last night alive.

Jane was a domestic servant. She had had employment previously in Wakefield but had just secured the job helping Mrs Hewitt, wife of the landlord of the public house, and had started work there only two days earlier. She had not wanted to ask for time off for the dance but Mrs Hewitt had encouraged her to go, saying that she could manage by herself after 10 pm. So Jane went back to the family home at 18 North's Yard, no great distance from *The Royal Oak*, got into her finery and by 11 pm was on the dance floor.

The Cricket Club whist drive and dance was an annual event and most of Crofton, perhaps especially the younger people, looked forward to it. It was held at the elementary school with the main hall being used as a ballroom. It was the time of the Crofton Feast and the school was closed for two days. By the time Jane got there the whist drive was over and dancing was in full swing.

Not far away, at the Working Men's Club, twenty-seven year old miner Edwin Sowerby was brooding over a glass of beer. Edwin lived close to Jane, at 3 North's Yard. He had been in love with her for long enough and for some time the two had been 'walking out' together. But earlier that year Jane had ended the relationship. Edwin was not prepared to take her 'no' for an answer.

Jane was described by Mrs Hewitt as a nice, cheerful girl, pleasant to everyone, a first-rate worker, willing and obliging. She was the eldest of five children. Sowerby was also held to

The Royal Oak *in Crofton where Jane Darwell obtained work shortly before her death.* The author

be a pleasant enough sort of chap – harmless and inoffensive. Sam Bateman, the checkweighman at Nostell Colliery, where Sowerby worked, spoke of him as 'as decent a young fellow as ever walked in the village'. But Dr G G Clarke thought that he was 'weak'.

At this time the miners were on strike. Perhaps Sowerby had too much time to dwell on Jane's rejection of him. Certainly on 8 October Dr Clarke had been called to his home where Sowerby lay in bed in a listless state complaining of pains in his head. Dr Clarke diagnosed neurasthenia – a nervous breakdown. That evening, or possibly the following one, Sowerby called at Jane's home. She was out but he told her parents that if he could not have her, then no one else would;

he would shoot her. Jane's father attributed his threats to the effects of drink and told him that he had 'better mind what he was doing'. Jane came in and Sowerby asked her outright if she loved him. She simply said, 'No'.

On 21 October the checkweighman encountered Sowerby who said that he was going to put his head on the railway line.

But he did not and on the fatal night of the Cricket Club dance, Sowerby made his way from the Working Men's Club to the school at about 11 pm. He was not a dancer.

Just after midnight, Jane was sitting out during the Lancers. On one side of her was Richard Sarson, the scorer for the cricket matches. On the other was another coalminer, Armitage Brook, from Nostell Row. Sowerby came across to them. He stooped as if to whisper in Jane's ear, then raised his right hand and brought it down, slashing Jane's throat with a razor. She gave a cry and then blood gushed in a torrent that covered Sarson's face so that for a moment he was blinded. Jane fell to the floor, blood still pouring from the wound. Sowerby turned the razor on himself but before he had inflicted more than a shallow wound, others seized and held

The elementary school in Crofton where the fatal dance was held. The author

him. Confusion reigned in the dance hall. The young people were said to have been 'terror struck' and women screamed at the sight of such a pool of blood on the floor.

James Redvers Allen, who had come from Sharlston for the dance and who knew Sowerby, went across to where he now lay on the floor and used his handkerchief to staunch the cut across the miner's throat. Sowerby asked him to feel in his pocket for his dance programme. Allen drew the card out and Sowerby asked him to read out what he had written on it. A pencilled message said, 'Me and Janie gone forever. E Sowerby. With love to all.'

Sergeant Anderson of the West Riding police arrived on the scene and took Sowerby to Clayton Hospital. Allen gave him the programme card. It was too late to do anything for Jane. When Dr Clarke arrived he found her stretched out on a bench. He said that she would have died instantly from so terrible a wound.

Jane's parents had gone to bed about midnight but had heard the screams from the dance hall and her father, Charles, had gone across to find the chilling sight of his murdered child. Jane's body was carried back to her home. Her funeral at Crofton parish church was taken on Thursday 28 October by the Rector, Reverend Henry Brownrigg. She was buried in the churchyard. The school remained closed for the remainder of the week. According to an account in *The History of Crofton* (2002), the bloodstained floorboards were taken up and replaced.

Sowerby remained in hospital for a week, watched over by policemen. He was then transferred to Armley gaol.

An inquest into Jane's death was opened on 27 October at the Primitive Methodist Chapel in Crofton and then adjourned until 4 November. It was there, with Sowerby present, handcuffed to prison warders and with a white muffler round his neck, that the whole wretched story came out. The inquest jury returned a verdict of wilful murder against Edwin Sowerby.

The charge against Sowerby was heard before West Riding magistrates at the Court House in Wakefield on 10 November. Here – and no doubt further imperilling the young man – Dr

Jane Darwell's grave at Crofton. Cynthia Dickinson.

Clarke at that time denied Sowerby having told him when he was ill that he had 'not slept for five weeks'.

Sowerby was committed for trial at the Assizes in Leeds. The case was heard on 9 December. His defence worked hard to convince the jury that he was not in his right mind when he struck at Jane. Sowerby had served in the army (after initially being rejected) from 1916–18 and had seen action in Ireland; his mother said that after his discharge he had regularly complained of head pains. However, Dr Clarke gave his view that the act was a matter of a 'momentary impulse' rather than 'temporary insanity' and that he knew what he was doing. He did admit that Sowerby's mother had told him that the young man had had little sleep during the five weeks before the day he had been called to attend to him, but he said that he would have 'known what he was doing' when he killed Jane. Dr Robert May, visiting physician at Clayton Hospital, confirmed that Sowerby was sane during his week's stay there. And there was clear evidence that the crime had been premeditated.

The jury found Sowerby guilty and the judge pronounced sentence of death.

Edwin Sowerby was hanged at Armley on 30 December by the official hangman. It was the fiftieth execution at the gaol.

CHAPTER 39

Death of a Wayward Wife
1923

At the initial hearing into the death of thirty-eight year old Elizabeth Beatrice Seaman, Coroner C J Haworth threatened to resume the inquest time after time until witnesses gave him a full and true account.

Elizabeth died in the White Rose Hospital (later the County General Hospital) in Wakefield on 2 June 1923. She had been taken there on 30 May from her home in Golden Square, Horbury, on the orders of Dr La Touche. Her husband of eleven years, farm labourer Arthur Seaman, said when the inquest opened at Wakefield Court House on 6 June that his wife had not been well for the previous six weeks but had become much worse on 29 May and, despite her protestations, he had called the doctor the following day. Other details came out about Elizabeth: she had had eight children, two even before her marriage, but six of the eight had died 'very young'. An unmarried sister, Annie Talbot, lived with the Seamans but Elizabeth was not on good terms with her other two sisters, Mary Ellen Taylor and Sarah Bland. None of this was especially shocking but Seaman then admitted that his wife had been in the habit of going off to Darton every Saturday to meet another man. Seaman had remonstrated with her but she insisted that she would do as she pleased. She had been in Darton on the Saturday before her death. He denied knowing what was wrong with his wife or to having seen any evidence that might shed light on her condition.

Elizabeth's married sisters also gave evidence at the first hearing. Sarah Bland lived in Melton Mowbray but had come up to Horbury on holiday and was with Mary Taylor at the latter's home in Ring o' Bells Yard, Horbury, when they heard on 30 May that Elizabeth was very ill. They had gone to the

Golden Square house before the ambulance arrived. Elizabeth had taken their hands, they said, and asked for their forgiveness to 'the great wrong' she had done. She had thrown a box of black pills on the table and she begged Mary to take the pills away and not let her husband see them. They claimed to have no idea what the pills were.

Mary's husband, however, fish and fruit hawker Robert Preston Taylor, told the coroner that he had had a pretty good idea what the pills were for and that he had thrown them on the fire before anyone else could come to harm from taking them.

The coroner has to adjourn the inquest only once. At the second hearing, on 27 June, Arthur Seaman was ready to provide more information and, indeed, to admit to having lied previously. Now he said that, in the early morning of 30 May,

The White Rose Hospital, later the County General Hospital, Wakefield, where Elizabeth Seaman died. Author's collection

he had gone downstairs to seek his wife as she had not come to bed. There was blood on newspapers on the kitchen floor. Two nurses from the White Rose Hospital said that Elizabeth had made no statement in the few days before her death. Dr Sutherland, however, was clear that his post-mortem examination showed that she had died from peritonitis following an abortion, but he had no means of knowing how it had been brought about.

The man from Darton gave evidence at the inquest and was allowed to remain unnamed. All he would say was that Elizabeth visited him occasionally but that he knew nothing of the cause of her death.

The inquest verdict was simply that Elizabeth had died from peritonitis following an abortion. No further blame was laid. But the coroner spoke very critically of the widower, Arthur Seaman, for earlier suppressing what he knew.

Chapter 40

The Best of Husbands
1927

Taking him all in all, Robert Lamb had been the best of husbands, his wife, May affirmed when he was tried for causing her grievous bodily harm.

The Lambs, who lived at 46 Manor Haigh Road on the then-new Lupset estate, Wakefield, had been married thirteen years and had three children when the incident occurred on Christmas Eve 1927. Lamb, a labourer, had been cleaning a couple of hats during the afternoon using petrol from a glass mineral-water bottle. During the afternoon the couple had exchanged hard words. May went out in the evening and did not return until 11pm. There was more argument and Lamb threw petrol from the bottle over his wife. What happened next is uncertain. The original account was that Lamb told May she

Houses in Manor Haigh Road, Lupset, where the Lambs lived. The author

was fit only to burn and that May seized a match and struck it and, saying, 'So burn I will,' was swiftly engulfed in the blaze. Lamb was distraught but had the sense to roll his wife in a rug to extinguish the flames. He called up the next-door neighbour, Alice Williams, a widow, about 12.15 am and asked her to see what she could for his wife. He was, according to Mrs Williams, quite demented, saying that he would 'go to the scaffold' for what had happened and searching the drawers for a razor. According to George Turnbull, who lodged with Mrs Williams, Lamb said that he had 'done it'.

Mrs Williams went for Nurse Mabel Bodkin, a midwife who lived at 2 Townley Road, who found May terribly burnt and the house in a dreadful disorder.

Someone telephoned the police office asking for an ambulance. This was driven to the house by Constable Ralph, and May was taken to Clayton Hospital where she was admitted at 1.30 am. Dr Charles Neville Robinson found severe burns to her head, face, neck, right arm, left wrist and the front of her chest. Lamb was arrested and charged with causing grievous bodily harm.

May survived. Lamb was brought before the Wakefield magistrates on 27 February 1928. Now the account of the incident was rather different. Both May and her husband agreed that they had had words and that Lamb had thrown petrol over her but it was 'only a drop'; there had been no more than an inch in the bottle and May had had no idea that that was what the liquid was. After the incident she had set about getting Lamb's supper and had then told him she was going to bed. It was only when she took a candle to the fire that the petrol ignited. Lamb, she said, had visited her in hospital and she was sure he would never have set fire to her himself.

Lamb confirmed that he and May had 'generally lived happily together'.

Lamb's solicitor, Catterall, asked for the charge to be reduced to one of common assault and to this the magistrates agreed. Lamb was fined £3 plus costs and bound over for two months.

CHAPTER 41

Murder at Bath Cottage
1928

Whatever prompted nineteen-year old Charles William Ward to make up a story about his father needing sand urgently from a firm in Barnsley, it did the young man little good. Despite his supposed alibi, he was convicted at Leeds Assizes in May 1928 of his father's murder.

The Ward family lived at Bath Cottage, Mill Lane, Ackworth, which Charles William Ward senior rented from Ackworth School. The house stood beside the Chalybeate bath, fed by a spring and used in the past as a swimming pool for the scholars. The elder Ward was a market gardener and his son worked as his assistant. Either one, or both, of the male Wards had had some employment also in scavenging but that contract had come to an end the previous May and the family's finances were, in March 1928, in a desperate situation. Ward junior, Willie as he was known, received only weekly pocket money of 3s 6d (17.5p) or sometimes 5s (25p). He was, it was alleged, very dissatisfied and 'sick of the way things were going on'. The household included Ward senior's second wife, Elizabeth, and the son of her marriage, twelve-year old Thomas Milner Ward. Willie was given to complaining about his step-mother's always wanting money.

On the morning of 28 March Mr Ward received a letter from Ackworth school demanding immediate payment of arrears of rent for the cottage. Mrs Ward planned to visit her niece in Beeston, Leeds, that morning and to negotiate the sale of the land attached to the cottage. She had only two shillings (10p) for her fare and the day's expenses and she sent Thomas out to the stable to ask his father for more money. The older boy was with his father at the time and claimed that his father had said he had no money to hand to give her. Thomas went off to school, Mrs Ward went off to Leeds, and her husband went

Bath Cottage, Ackworth, now known as Bath House, where Charles William Ward senior was murdered. The author

into Pontefract where he drew £1 from the bank and collected 7s 6d (37.5p) that was owed to him.

Ward senior was seen returning home soon after one o'clock. According to Willie, Ward had brought a pick-axe into the cottage saying that he was going to chop some wood and lay a fire. He left the axe in the scullery. The two then had lunch together. The young man was seen at about 2.15 pm hurrying to catch the bus to Barnsley. What else happened in the hour that father and son were together in the house can have been known only by them and when Thomas returned from school at 4.10 pm the father was dead.

Willie claimed that his father had sent him to Barnsley to tell a Mr Birch to send a quantity of sand at once. His father had given him 2s 6d (12.5p) for the trip and had come to the gate to see him off. The last he saw of him, he said, was chasing a stray hen off the road. At 3.30 pm, presumably for no reason other than to strengthen his alibi, Willie called at Holgate Grammar School, Barnsley, where he saw the caretaker, Herbert Arthur Creighton, and asked him whether he would like sand delivering from a firm in York. Creighton replied that any sand was sent to the school under contract by a Barnsley firm.

If Willie killed his father – and the juries both at the inquest and at the Assizes were convinced that he had done – then it was a further callous act to leave the discovery of the murder to his young half-brother. Returning from school at 4.10 pm, Thomas found the front door of the cottage – unusually – locked and went in through the back one. There he saw an ominous bundle on the sofa with the handle of a pick-axe lying against the sofa head. He climbed on a chair and unbolted the front door and went to look for his step-brother. He saw the schoolmaster, Mr Robinson, pass in the lane but was too frightened to speak to him. When Willie arrived home at about 4.20 pm, Thomas told him that 'something had happened'. They went into the cottage together. Willie did not, at that time, touch anything. He claimed later that he recognised the body of his father, hidden under blankets and cushions, by his boots. They hurried out again and Willie asked a neighbour, Ronald Desborough, to call a doctor and the police as his father had been murdered.

Willie had already attempted to provide himself with an alibi. Now he tried hard – too hard – to throw the blame for his father's death on others. When Dr W F Royston arrived at about 4.45 pm, Willie took him into the house and pointed to the heap on the sofa. Royston uncovered the corpse and found a pick-axe embedded to a depth of four and a half inches into the skull. Willie then drew attention to papers scattered both in the living room and in his father's bedroom, suggesting that there had been a burglary. Later he told the police that his father had sent him to Barnsley to get him out of the way because he was expecting a visitor or visitors and did not want him to know. Yet he admitted that he had bolted the front door himself and said that this was because his father was absent minded and he did not want him to wander out.

Then Willie reported a conversation he had, supposedly, had with his aunt, Mrs Laura Bowman, some three years previously: she was alleged to have warned him that his father would kill his step-mother 'same as he killed your own mother'. Perhaps now he wished to imply that his step-mother was involved in the murder.

When Mrs Ward arrived home at 7.20 pm she was met at the gate of the cottage by the Chief Constable of the West Riding and was taken to a neighbour's. She then went to stay with Mrs Bowman, in Ropergate, Pontefract. Closely questioned at the inquest into her husband's death, she said that she avoided contact with Willie because if she spoke to him she would have asked directly why he did it. There was no doubt in her mind as to the identity of the murderer. Moreover, she added, there had been no need for her husband to bring a pick-axe into the house: they had a small axe for chopping wood.

The inquest, a two-day hearing in Pontefract on 17 and 18 April, learned that, after extensive inquiries, the police concluded that no strangers had been seen in Ackworth on the afternoon of Ward's death and no one had called at Bath Cottage. Mrs Bowman denied ever having uttered any warning to Willie about his father. Ward told of his fruitless journey to Barnsley but the coroner questioned why Ward, who was desperately short of money, would give the young man 2s 6d (12.5p) to go on a wild-goose chase. Walter Birch, a contractor of Stockton Lane, York, said that as it happened he had passed though Ackworth on 28 March but he did not know Mr Ward and had never had an order from him for sand. Had Willie simply seen the name on a vehicle and woven it into his tissue of lies?

In summing up, the coroner said that no one had had the opportunity to murder Ward except his son. It took the jury some time to reach a verdict but finally they agreed that Willie had murdered his father.

Willie was arrested immediately. Once in custody he told a new story. His step-mother had taken him aside on the day before Ward died, and had told him that she had a wealthy man friend called Fred. He alleged that she said, 'If your father was out of the way, we should all be well off. I shall try to get Fred to do something to him.' Willie now embellished the story. When he went to Barnsley on the afternoon of Ward's death, he thought Fred was 'in the small yard underneath the pig places' and that he had 'had an idea' that Fred was going to kill his father.

At Willie's trial at the Assizes, Mrs Ward strongly denied ever having told Willie of any friend. Willie himself chose – or was well advised – not to give evidence. In the end it was the forensic evidence rather than his lies that convicted him. The County Pathologist, Dr P L Sutherland, who had performed an autopsy, said that Ward's stomach contained potato in the early stages of digestion; he must have died within an hour of eating his lunch. If the meal was at 1.15 pm, he would have been dead by the time Willie was seen on his way to catch the bus to Barnsley. The findings were confirmed by the Home Office pathologist, Sir Bernard Spilsbury.

Willie was convicted and sentenced to death. His solicitors sought leave to appeal on the grounds that there was insufficient evidence for a conviction and that the summing up had been unsatisfactory. On 11 June the Court of Criminal Appeal rejected the application.

However, at the end of the month news came that the sentence had been commuted by the Home Secretary to one of penal servitude for life.

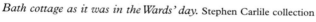

Bath cottage as it was in the Wards' day. Stephen Carlile collection

CHAPTER 42

Whose Razor Was It?
1929

Both John Cock and Winifred Pollard died from throat wounds made by a white-handled razor which was found on a table close to their bodies. We can never know, however, which of the fatal pair inflicted the first gash or what led up to the violence in the early hours of Monday 15 July 1929.

John William Cock, a gasworks labourer, who was forty-three and a widower, lived at 21 Warrengate with his two younger children, Walter and Lily. His elder son, Wilfred, was a private in the East Kent regiment. Winifred Pollard was thirty-seven and lived with her daughter Mary at her parents' home in Sun Lane. She had been married in 1919 to a Blackpool barman but the relationship had lasted only six years.

Evidence given at the inquest on 18 July showed that after his wife's death in 1929. Cock had become depressed and had struck up some kind of friendship with Pollard. The two had enjoyed a drink together and had been to the cinema at least once. But until the night of her death, Pollard had never, according to his children, been in Cock's house.

It was the children who first saw the horrible scene. Lily and Walter had been out during the Sunday evening but had come home and gone to bed about 10.30 pm. At that time their father was alone downstairs. Lily had been woken from her sleep by a thud. She had gone to her brother's room and the two of them had lit a candle and crept down the stairs. Seeing the bodies they had retreated to a bedroom and opened the window to call for help.

It was about 1.45 in the morning when Police Constable Dale heard their cries. He sent for Dr Robinson who confirmed that Pollard, who was clutching some coins in her

Sun Lane where Winifred Pollard lived with her mother prior to her death.
The author

right hand, had been dead for about an hour. Cock was still alive and was taken to Clayton Hospital. For a short time he rambled, saying, 'She did it,' but he died at 4.30 am. But, whilst Pollard might have brought the razor to the house and struck the first blow, injuring Cock, there was no way, according to Dr Robinson, that she could have killed herself.

Pollard's mother, Elizabeth Rayner, admitted at the inquest that her daughter had a violent temper. She had been furious with Cock on Sunday evening, saying to her mother that, 'The old devil is not going out tonight but that will not stop me'. She had left home at 7.30 pm, returned at 9.40 pm, gone out again ostensibly to get some beer and never returned to Sun Lane.

Ivy Northern, of 2 Gas House Yard, told the inquest that she had known the Cocks for fifteen years and that since Mrs Cock's death she had done some cooking for them. She had never seen Pollard in Cock's house and she had never seen the white-handled razor there either. Lily Cock was evidently keen to clear her father's name and assured the inquest that the razor was not one of his.

But even if Pollard had come to the Warrengate house with the razor, she could not have inflicted the wound that killed her. Dr Robinson was clear that it had been dealt by a right hand, yet her right hand was still clutching some coins. Moreover it would have required far more strength than she could have had. The incident might have begun by Pollard striking Cock, however. His cut was far less deep and he might then have seized the razor and attacked her.

The jury was not impressed. They concluded that Cock had both killed Pollard and inflicted the injuries on himself.

CHAPTER 43

Grave Suspicions
1937

There might be grave suspicions as to how little Patsy Austin came to drown, Coroner C J Haworth told the inquest jury, but grave suspicions are not enough unless they can be proved up to the hilt. Very possible Patsy was murdered by her mother, but the verdict at the inquest on 21 March 1937 could be no more than 'found drowned'.

Patsy was a mere fifteen months old when she died. Her little body was taken from the River Calder at Newmarket colliery staithe on 10 March. Her mother, twenty-four year old Irene Austin was nowhere to be found.

Irene and her husband, Harry, a colliery fitter, lived in lodgings at 22 Saville Street, Wakefield, with their three children, Patsy, and two older boys. In March Irene knew that she was pregnant again. In the early evening of Tuesday 9 March, Harry and Irene had an argument. Harry went out at about 6.30 pm without telling his wife where he was going. Irene shouted after him from the bedroom window, 'I am going to do it.' Whatever Harry may have understood by that, he continued on his way. When he returned about 9 pm, both Irene and Patsy were gone. The landlady told him that Irene had said that she was going to visit Harry's mother at Bottomboat. That evening he made no move to fetch her home or to report her missing. She had left home before, he later explained. When the police arrived to question him the next day after Patsy's body had been found, he said that he had been about to go to Bottomboat just then to look for Irene and the little girl.

The police thought it probable that Irene too was dead. She had been seen with Patsy on a bus going to Bottomboat and had been seen there walking towards the river. The river, which was in flood after two weeks of heavy rain, was dragged. Divers and even a diviner were brought in to search for her body. But a description was circulated in the hope that she might still be found alive: she was five feet six or seven tall, well built, with dark bobbed hair, brown eyes, a fresh complexion and good teeth.

Meanwhile an inquest was opened at the *Commercial Inn*, Methley, on Friday 12 March on the body of little Patsy. When it resumed on 21 March, it was reported that her mother was still missing.

It was not until 7 April that Irene's body was found in the River Aire close to Ferrybridge power station. She was dragged from the water by an auxiliary attendant there, Clifford Pease Firth of 10 Crewe Avenue, Ferrybridge. There

The staithe at Newmarket Colliery where Patsy's body was found. The John Goodchild Collection.

was a brief hearing at Pontefract on 9 April when Harry Austin identified the body as that of his wife. When the inquest resumed on 20 April, The West Riding pathologist, Dr P L Sutherland, said that death was by drowning and there was nothing about the body to suggest foul play; it might well have been in the water for a month. Harry admitted that there had been an argument but the coroner refused to allow him to be questioned about its nature, insisting that quarrels between husbands and wives were not relevant. The coroner also ruled out any insights that might be had from the inquest into Patsy's death. The sole business of the hearing was to establish the cause of Irene's death. Harry said that his wife had never threatened suicide and had left no note. However the jury returned a verdict of suicide during a fit of temporary insanity.

We can only speculate on the stress that led Irene to kill her little girl and herself. Was it the distress at the prospect of a fourth child? How difficult had it been for her, with three children already, to cope with the family in lodgings? Or had a deteriorating relationship with her husband led to the deaths? There is no evidence to provide answers.

The River Aire at Ferrybridge where Irene's body was found. Simon Jenkins

CHAPTER 44

Irrational Jealousy
1945

His neighbour believed that Cyril Moore had seemed to be 'going queer' in the weeks in 1945 before he killed his wife and then took his own life, but the inquest jury decided that there was insufficient evidence to show his state of mind. What seems certain is that he killed her in a jealous rage prompted by his belief that she was entertaining other men, or more particularly their neighbour, at their home at the Lock, Altofts, on the Aire and Calder Navigation.

Moore was thirty-six and had been employed as an embankment repairer and lock-keeper by the Navigation

Woodnook lock and lock house, Altofts, in 2003. Joshua Taylor, whom Cyril Moore suspected of visiting his wife, lived here. Simon Jenkins.

authority. He and his thirty-four year old wife, Annie, had five children, the eldest of them, who was seventeen, having been brought up by his grandparents.

Some time in the early summer Moore had gone to the nearby house of Joshua Taylor at Woodnook Lock, with his eyes 'glaring', Taylor said, and had warned him to 'keep out of my house' and knocked him out. Taylor claimed that he had lain unconscious for twenty minutes. At the inquest into the two deaths, Taylor said that he had been inside the Moores' house only once although he did regularly go there to fill a water tank from an outside tap.

Shortly after this incident, Moore had accused his wife of adultery and threatened her with a knife. She had run from the house and gone for refuge to her brother, John Thomas Corfield, who lived at 13 Altofts Road, Normanton. Her younger children had moved in there with her.

Moore became a regular visitor to Corfield's house, sometimes staying overnight with his wife. He gave up his job with the Navigation company and talked of moving to York. It seemed possible that Annie would decide to go with him. Certainly Corfield thought that the couple were getting along quite well together again.

On the evening of 28 July, Corfield went to the cinema leaving Moore and Annie in the house. One of their daughters was taking part in a dancing display that evening and fifteen-year old Evelyn said at the inquest into their deaths that her parents had gone out together intending to watch it. The couple were next seen at about 10.30 pm in the *Royal Engineers Inn* in Carlton Street, Castleford. Annie was heard to say, 'It looks like us walking home'. Cyril seemed to agree and they set off together in the direction of Normanton.

They never got there. In the small hours of the morning, Joseph Hudson, who was a signal-man with the LMS railway at Altofts, heard running footsteps passing his box. As he walked home at 3.45 am he stumbled across a body on the line. Both its head and its legs had been completely severed. It was later identified, by its new boots, as that of Cyril Moore.

That afternoon Marjorie Lyle, of 449 Casteford Road, Normanton, who was on leave from the ATS prior to discharge, took a group of local children for a walk in the fields at Whitwood. There she discovered the body of Annie Moore. She quickly got the children away before reporting what she had found to the police.

The short inquest held immediately to identify the bodies was resumed at the Court House in Castleford on 31 August.. Harold Macauley, of Heron Grove, Normanton, said that at about 1.20am on Sunday morning, as he and his wife were walking home, he saw a man resembling Moore on his own coming from the carriageway near the *Good Hope Inn*. The carriageway led to the field where Annie's body was found. The county pathologist, Professor Sutherland, said that Annie had died from being strangled. The jury decided that Annie had been murdered by her husband and that he had committed suicide but that there was not enough evidence to show his state of mind.

CHAPTER 45

Buried in a Slag Heap
1953

If it had not been for an astute benefits clerk, perhaps the murder of little Margaret Walker would never have come to light.

Margaret was the illegitimate daughter of Barbara Peacock Walker and had been born on 10 June 1952. Her father was Jugoslavian. The child seems to have been handicapped for, by the time she was seventeen or eighteen months old, she could neither walk nor crawl.

A few months after Margaret's birth, Barbara met lorry driver Clarence Walter Ward in Wakefield. The two became an 'item' and moved in together, with baby Margaret, in a room in Hillary Street, Leeds.

It was there, in November or December 1953, that Ward killed Margaret. He had been violent with the child before. Margaret cried a good deal and Barbara later said that he used to hit her with his hand or even hold his hand over her mouth to stop her breathing.

On the fatal evening, Ward came home from work demanding his tea. Margaret was lying on the bed but the bedstead was broken and Ward and Barbara lifted the mattress onto the floor under the window so that he could do some repairs. Margaret was put on the mattress to play. Ward then sent Barbara out to the local shop for some cigarettes. When she got back, her baby was lying dead on the floor near the grate. At first Ward said that she had crawled off the mattress and fallen, but Barbara knew that that was impossible. She said that she would call a doctor so that he could find out how Margaret had died. But Ward threatened to kill her if she called either a doctor or the police.

About 8 o'clock that evening, the couple set out by tram to Belle Isle, Leeds. Ward was carrying the baby, carefully wrapped round as if she were asleep. They walked down Sharpe Lane to Robin Hood. Here Ward tried to dig a hole in a field but the ground was so hard that the shovel broke. The wretched pair walked on to Rothwell Haigh Colliery and here Ward stripped the child and buried it under some rocks in a slag heap at Rose Pit. Back at their lodging, Ward burned the baby's clothes.

Were questions asked about the baby by the neighbours? Certainly soon afterwards Ward and Barbara Walker moved to Horbury. Here, in March 1955, the banns were called for their wedding. But within a few days of the date they were to be married, Ward walked out. Four days later he was married to another woman. He and his wife went to live in Edlington, near Doncaster. Barbara Walker remained in Horbury.

It was in August 1955 that Barbara hurt her thumb at work and claimed National Assistance. She was asked to go to Pontefract for an interview. There, the clerk asked her about the child for whom she had claimed benefit two years earlier. Barbara said that the little girl had been taken away by Ward and she had not seen her again. But the clerk was suspicious and reported the matter to the police.

Rose Pit, Rothwell Haigh, where Barbara Walker's baby was buried. The John Goodchild Collection.

Walker and Ward took a tram to Belle Isle on their way to dispose of the dead baby. The last Leeds trams ran in 1959. Norman Ellis collection

Barbara was interviewed on 28 August by Inspector Charles Byrne. It was then that the dreadful story was revealed. Byrne went to see Ward. At first he claimed that the baby had gone to live with Barbara's sister in London and that, when he had last seen her, little Margaret was alive and well. But as the questioning continued, he admitted shaking the little girl and that she had died. He was arrested and charged with murder.

The next day, the police began their search for the child's body. It took two days of digging and the removal of several hundred tons of slag before the decayed remains were found. Professor C J Polson of Leeds University Department of Forensic Medicine said that the baby's skull had been crushed on both sides as if gripped very tightly.

Appearing before Leeds City magistrates, Ward was committed for trial at the Assizes. The case was heard in Leeds in December 1955 and he was found guilty and sentenced to death. An appeal was turned down by the Lord Chief Justice on 11 January 1956 and the date of execution was set for 26 January.

By the mid 1950s there was considerable opposition to the death penalty which was suspended in 1965 and finally abolished. Ward's wife campaigned energetically in the days after the appeal was dismissed. She wrote to the Queen and to her M P, Tom Williams. She got up a petition to the Home Secretary. Ward himself wrote to the Home Secretary. Just seventy-two hours before he was to be hung, Ward was reprieved.

CHAPTER 46

Left to Die in a Haystack
1954

Exactly what was in Rose Edge's mind when she abandoned her fourteen-week old baby in an isolated haystack somewhere between Walton and Wintersett? She was charged with attempting to murder the child by abandoning it and alternatively with abandoning the child and thus endangering its life. When she appeared before the West Riding magistrates on 3 March 1954, the prosecution claimed that there must have been 'murder in her heart'.

Edge was one of seven children. Her family had lived at West Lodge, Walton Hall, until 1950, and had then moved to Linghouse Farm, Stainforth, near Doncaster. Edge had worked as a probationer nurse at Walton Hall at a time when it was a maternity hospital, but had then been employed as a receptionist at hotels in Blackpool and Morecambe. Pregnant, she returned to Stainforth. Her daughter, Hilda Virginia Edge, was born in a Doncaster nursing home on 8 November 1953. Edge claimed that she was married to its father, whom she named as Russell Edge, and that he was a Canadian student of architecture. She also claimed that he had deserted her and that he had been drowned at sea.

Possibly much of what the young woman said was untrue. But what was she to do? There must have seemed little option but to give the baby up for adoption. Edge got in touch with the Doncaster Child Adoption Society saying that she wanted the child adopted because she had neither the time nor the money to bring her up herself. She was asked for her marriage certificate. When she failed to produce it, the Society rejected the application.

Edge must have been desperate. On the afternoon of Monday 15 February 1954, she set out from her parents' home with the baby, telling her mother that she was going to the Adoption Society's office to meet a woman from Leeds who would adopt baby Hilda. Instead she took a bus to Walton. As it chanced, she encountered someone who knew her, Mrs Dunn, who herself lived in Walton, recognized her and started to chat. Edge told her that the baby was her sister's. At six o'clock that evening, Edge left the baby in the haystack.

And there the child might well have died. Yet Hilda survived two wintry nights and a wintry day. On the morning of Wednesday 17 February, sixteen-year old Brian Dodd, of Mulberry Place, Ryhill, heard cries which at first he thought were those of a rabbit. Finding the baby, he took her straight to the home of Mrs Doreen Ayrton at Reservoir Cottage, Wintersett. She was in a pathetic state – wet, cold and hungry. Mrs Ayrton sent for Dr David Vining from Ryhill and meanwhile changed the child and fed her. Dr Vining said that the baby could not have lived much longer if Brian had not found her.

When the police called at Edge's home, she denied ever having been in Walton and insisted that her baby had been

West Lodge, Walton Hall, in 2003. The author

adopted. Eventually, she admitted abandoning the child but swore that she had never meant to kill her. However, acting for the prosecution, Maurice Shaffner asked whether, having left the baby at so isolated a spot, she could ever have intended anything else.

Edge was committed for trial at Leeds Assizes. Unusually, her solicitor asked that she be kept in custody, telling the court that she was happy in prison.

No report of a trial has been found. It may be, of course, that the Grand Jury decided that there was some doubt over whether a jury would convict her on the charge of attempted murder and decided to drop the case. As for baby Hilda, she was placed in the care of the local authority.

CHAPTER 47

Another Open Verdict
1955

Aman of Colonel Thomas Chadwick's 'calibre and record' would never take his own life while of sound mind. So said the Coroner B W Little at the inquest into Chadwick's death which was held in Dewsbury on Saturday 16 July, 1955. Yet there were clear indications in the evidence that the distinguished officer and public figure might well have intended to drown himself.

Chadwick was a director of the family firm of T Chadwick and Sons Ltd, wool merchants, of Eastfield Mill, Dewsbury. He had served in the first world war and had won the Military Cross at Passchendaele. Much involved in the Territorial Army, he had for some years been the Honorary Colonel of the fourth battalion of the Kings Own Yorkshire Light Infantry, and was still the Colonel Commander of the West Riding Army Cadet Force. He was a director of Wakefield Building Society and of Wakefield Golf Club. In 1949 he had been made a Deputy Lieutenant of the West Riding. He had become a Wakefield magistrate in 1944 and at the time of his death was the Chairman of the Bench. He was, said fellow Justice of the Peace Eric Stonehouse, one of the kindest and most genial of men, yet a firm and fearless magistrate. He was sixty-one. He lived with his wife, Nora, or 'Lulu', at Hesselwood, Manygates Lane, Wakefield. The couple had no children.

On 12 July Chadwick drove to Dewsbury and spent the first part of the morning at the mill He chatted in his office to his nephew, Arthur Charles Chadwick, who was the mill manager. They discussed, it was later said, routine work matters. They were joined by Colonel Chadwick's brother, Herbert Marriott Chadwick. Both men said at the inquest that the Colonel had seemed worried, although not unduly distressed. He had talked about another brother, who was blind, and a sister, who was in hospital.

About 10.50 am, John Armstead, the works foreman, saw Colonel Chadwick who, he said, seemed 'perfectly normal'. A little while later he was seen by Ronald Mooney, a warehouseman, in the doorway of the willeying shop. The Colonel then did something that Mooney had never seen before: he walked out of the main gates and turned down Sands Lane. He was never seen alive again.

The alarm was raised that evening when it was realised that Chadwick's car was still at the mill and his wife reported that he had not returned home. Both police and members of the army were engaged in looking for him.

Chadwick was found two days later. Police Constable Malcolm Smith was at the rear of the premises of Mason Bros, Smelters, in Mill Street East, Dewsbury, when he saw Chadwick's body lying in the River Calder on top of the weir. The corpse was fully clothed even to his shoes.

So how did Chadwick drown? The coroner asked a great many questions both of the pathologist and of the Colonel's

The Sands Lane entrance to Chadwick and Sons' mill, where Colonel Chadwick was last seen alive. The author

family. Dr Maurice Corridan, who had examined the body, said that the immediate cause of death was asphyxia due to drowning. But there was evidence of severe arteriosclerosis, the arteries were 'grossly diseased' and it was certainly possible that Chadwick could have had a heart attack and staggered into the river.

Arthur Chadwick said that his uncle's health was 'not too good' and that he had had trouble with his legs and had some difficulty walking. However, he had never complained about having any attack of cramp. Both Arthur and Herbert Chadwick insisted that he had never threatened to take his own life.

Constable Smith said that there were places on Sands Lane where it would have been possible to fall into the river.

When Chadwick's body was recovered, his pockets were found to contain only a green fountain pen, a gold cigarette case which was empty, and a box of matches. What else would he normally have had with him? After the body was found, Herbert Chadwick had searched his brother's office and had found, in the safe, his silver watch, a gold chain, his wallet and cheque book, his diary and some small change. He agreed that the Colonel would have had some of these items with him when he came over to Dewsbury on the morning he disappeared. Why had he taken them from his pockets? But there was no letter explaining his intentions. However, Herbert Chadwick admitted that his brother did not normally take a walk by the river.

The coroner suggested that there could have been rational reasons for Chadwick's having put the articles in the safe, though he did not elaborate as to what these might have been. If the jury were uncertain as to how Chadwick came to drown, they must record an open verdict. They did so.

Chadwick's funeral was a splendid affair. It took place at St Helen's Church, Sandal, on Monday 18 July. The Provost of Wakefield, Canon Noel T Hopkins, read the lessons and led the prayers. The Bishop of Wakefield, Dr Roger P Wilson, gave the address. The Mayor of Wakefield was present as were six Deputy Lieutenants of the County. The coffin was carried by nine officers of the fourth battalion of the KOYLI.

CHAPTER 48

The 'Mouse' Who Stabbed Her Husband
1982

In thirty-three years of marriage, Elsie Swift had become 'downtrodden, timid, cowering' and almost like a mouse. She was so afraid of her husband, Ernest, that when the price of her regular items of groceries went up, she would borrow money from a neighbour rather than tell him that she had spent more than he expected. The last few years of marriage had become worse than ever: her daughter – her one source of affection and support – had died in childbirth in 1978. Elsie never got over her death. Ernest had retired a year later and she had to endure his ceaseless presence in the house. Then in 1981 he had had a slight stroke, chose do little for himself and exerted further tyranny. He was, it was said at Elsie's trial, 'demanding, dictatorial and increasingly very very selfish'. Elsie became increasingly isolated, virtually a prisoner in her own home and, after her daughter's death 'deprived of those small kindnesses and comforts that make life bearable'.

On Saturday morning, 13 March, 1982 police were called to the couple's home, 21 Dent Drive, Wakefield. They found the body of sixty-seven year old Ernest lying in the hallway behind the front door. He had been stabbed repeatedly. At first Elsie denied all knowledge of what had happened; Ernest's wallet was missing and police thought that there had been a robbery but Elsie had taken the wallet herself and hidden it. A further interview with her the next day resulted in her confession.

It was a pathetic story. On the morning of his death, Elsie went out to buy a paper and then sat reading it to him. Ernest suffered from chronic constipation and demanded that Elsie insert a suppository into his anus. When this had no effect he insisted that Elsie call an ambulance. She thought he was worrying unnecessarily but offered to fetch a doctor. He persisted in demanding an ambulance and, provoked beyond endurance, Elsie seized the nearest weapon, a pair of scissors, and drove them into his chest.

Elsie was arrested and brought before the magistrates. She was charged with murder and taken to Risley remand centre. There was concern about her mental condition and at a further hearing, on 29 April, she was granted bail on condition that she live at Waddislove Hospital, Bradford, where a psychiatrist, Dr Peter Wood, would observe her condition and determine whether she was suffering from a depressive illness.

The short trial was held at Leeds Crown Court on 28 July. Elsie pleaded not guilty to murder but guilty to manslaughter on the grounds of provocation. Her plea was accepted. The prosecuting counsel described her as a vulnerable personality and a neurotic woman with emotional problems who had been treated for some years for her 'nerves'. Her defending counsel spoke of her as decent and timid. Her husband, however, was a cantankerous man who must have been difficult to live with.

At the end of the trial, the judge observed, 'Although this isn't murder, you must realise you have to be punished for killing your husband.' He sentenced Elsie to three years' imprisonment.

CHAPTER 49

The Bones Were Not For
Use in His Work
1986

Dental lecturer Samson Perera insisted that the bones found in a coffee jar in his laboratory at Leeds University Dental School were specimens needed for his work. But it was impossible to maintain that the one hundred and fifty pieces of bone that were retrieved from the coffee jar, from his home and from an envelope in a desk drawer were really being kept innocently for his research as an oral biologist.

The courts decided that they were the remains of Perera's adopted daughter, Nilanthie, and in March 1986 he was sentenced to life imprisonment for her murder.

Stillwell Drive, Sandal, Wakefield, where Natalie's remains were found at the Pereras' home. The author

Perera and his wife, Dammika, lived with their two children at 16 Stillwell Drive, Sandal, Wakefield. Both came from Sri Lanka. The couple met when Perera, who had gained a commonwealth scholarship, was at Newcastle University and Dammika was studying at the further education college there. They were married in 1973. In 1976 Dammika gained a teachers' certificate and worked as a Maths teacher before the couple's two children were born.

It was in 1981 that Perera, visiting his parents in Sri Lanka, adopted ten-year old Nilanthie, a member of a poor family living in the jungle. The little girl came to England that December.

But after a call by a health visitor on December 1983, Nilanthie was never seen again. Friends who asked Dammika about the girl were given evasive answers. Then, in July 1984 the contents of an anonymous letter sent to the Wakefield Social Services Department prompted a police investigation. Inspector Tom Hodgson and Detective Sergeant Kevin Woodford called on the Pereras. They were told that Nilanthie had never settled in England and been taken to Sicily, where Perera's brother lived, and that from there she would have been taken back to Sri Lanka. The police were dissatisfied and on 30 December Perera was questioned more closely. He then said that he had bought tickets for both himself and Nilanthie from Pickford's in Leeds for the flight to Sicily. The travel agent was able to confirm that Perera had bought a ticket for himself and flown to Catania on 10 April 1984 but he had never booked a ticket for a child. Perera then said that, as Nilanthie was a minor, he had not bought a ticket for her at all but that he had definitely taken her with him. The idea that a girl of Nilanthie's age could travel on his knee and without a ticket was rejected by the police as entirely absurd. Perera was lying.

It seems that after Nilanthie's death – and exactly when and how it took place was never determined – her body was buried in the garden of the Stillwell Grove house but as the police became more suspicious, Perera exhumed it and began to try to dispose of it piece by piece. Some of the forensic evidence was revolting: maggots had been found in the earth behind the

Pereras' garage; similar maggots had been found beneath the floor boards in their house, suggesting that the body had been moved from the former place to the latter.

On 4 February 1986 a colleague at the Dental School was horrified to find human bones in a coffee jar and a beaker and he contacted the police. A search revealed further bones in the envelope in Perera's desk. Perera and his wife were arrested the same day, charged initially with obstructing the coroner in the execution of his duty. Their house was searched and more bones, and in some instances chunks of flesh too, were found in plant pots, in a container under the kitchen sink, in a margarine tub, and in a bloodstained holdall in the loft.

Perera insisted that the items were all part of a cadaver that he had brought from Sri Lanka for his teaching. However, Professor Alan Usher, head of the Department of Pathology at Sheffield University, was clear that the remains were those of a girl aged between twelve and fifteen and that they had been buried some six months before their discovery. Moreover, the bones at the dental laboratory were in a dish containing decalcifying fluid – intended to dissolve them – whereas bones required as specimens for teaching would have been in a preservative. Then, Perera's former professor in Sri Lanka, confirmed that Perera had not obtained any corpse there.

Perera and Dammika were tried at Leeds Crown Court in February and March 1986. Professor Usher told the court that it was impossible to say how Natalie had died and that she could have died from natural causes. It was impossible to know whether either Perera or his wife had killed the child or, if they had, what their motive was. In Dammika's defence, it was claimed that Perera was a dominating husband who treated his wife like a little girl. The prosecution agreed that in Sri Lanka women were expected to be subservient to their husbands but that that did not exonerate them in Britain.

Dammika was found guilty of assisting her husband and was given a twelve month suspended sentence enabling her to care for the couple's children.

Index

INDEX OF PLACES